JACKSON VERSUS BIDDLE
THE STRUGGLE OVER THE
SECOND BANK OF THE
UNITED STATES

Problems in American Civilization

UNDER THE EDITORIAL DIRECTION OF
George Rogers Taylor

Jackson versus Biddle

THE STRUGGLE OVER THE
SECOND BANK OF THE UNITED STATES

EDITED WITH AN INTRODUCTION BY

George Rogers Taylor

Problems in American Civilization

READINGS SELECTED BY THE
DEPARTMENT OF AMERICAN STUDIES
AMHERST COLLEGE

D. C. HEATH AND COMPANY: Boston

INTRODUCTION

ALONE among the great nations of the world the United States still lacks a highly centralized banking system. The reasons for this are largely historical; they stem from the struggle over the attempt to recharter the second Bank of the United States. The bitterness of that controversy and the fear and hatred of the second Bank were such that only very slowly and with the greatest reluctance has this country permitted the creation of something approaching a central banking institution.

Following the expiration of the charter of the second Bank of the United States in 1836 the state banks were entirely on their own. The Independent Treasury System of the federal government, established in 1846 (it also existed for a brief period in 1840–1841), was little more than a receiving and disbursing instrument for the federal treasury. But in connection with the need for funds during the Civil War, and also to bring about a safer and more uniform currency, the National Banking System was inaugurated in 1864. Particularistic and without central direction, this system, though it brought about improved currency conditions, proved inadequate to meet those situations which required financial leadership and concerted action. Only after fifty years and a succession of serious financial crises were old prejudices against central direction sufficiently overcome to permit the establishment of the Federal Reserve System in

1914. And even then the system established was not *unitary* but *federal*, and a serious attempt was made to avoid giving complete power over its operations either to private business or to the federal government.

The beginnings of this struggle which has had such a lasting effect on our financial institutions go back to the first years of our national history, when the Federalists under the leadership of Hamilton secured the chartering of the first Bank of the United States. This institution, modeled after the Bank of England, was regarded by the dominant merchant class of that time as a financial institution necessary to the orderly and efficient functioning of both public and private business. To the agrarians led by Jefferson and to their chief spokesman, John Taylor of Caroline, it was an instrument of concentrated power threatening the interests of farmers and planters. Alarm over the threat of the Bank died down somewhat after the Anti-Federalists came into power, but when the charter expired in 1811 it was not renewed.

The history of the second Bank of the United States is briefly traced in the first of the readings contained in this volume. This is followed by a set of documents contemporary with the great struggle between Jackson and the Bank. Jackson's veto message is perhaps the best-known presidential veto in our history. The reply by Daniel Webster represents the well-considered view of the chief spokesman for the forces favoring recharter. Far less restraint characterizes many of the numerous other attacks on Jackson's action; the two newspaper editorials next reprinted are typical of the almost hysterical reaction of a large part of the press. The last of the contemporary items, a letter written by the historian George Bancroft, illustrates the depth of popular feeling against the bank; it is the Jacksonian reply to such statements as Webster's speech and the editorials which precede it in this volume.

Far from ending in the 1830's, the Bank War has continued down to the present day, resulting in an ever-growing volume of writing not unevenly balanced between the defenders and the attackers. The former are given their day in court by the inclusion of two items: the first is from the pen of the able historian of the Bank, Ralph C. H. Catterall, who fifty years ago wrote what is still recognized as the most detailed and authoritative study of that institution, and the second is an article by Bray Hammond, perhaps the most able and vigorous of present-day defenders of the second Bank. Opposed to these stands the work of Arthur M. Schlesinger, Jr., from whose Pulitzer Prize-winning book, *The Age of Jackson*, four chapters have been included. Many of the reviews of this book were very favorable indeed, but a dissenting one, a critical composition by Hammond, has been included as the final reading because it specifically raises the bank issue and permits a brief, last word to the proponents of the Bank in this more than a century of controversy.

In the choice of these readings one issue, the constitutionality of the institution, has been slighted. Though regarded as of the greatest moment at the time, this aspect of the problem has declined in interest for modern readers. One issue has been stressed, the danger believed by many to result from the concentration of great economic power in the hands of a few men not directly responsible to the people for their behavior. The problems arising in this connection — especially those having to do with the relations of private finance and business to the state — are as contemporary as today and tomorrow and as fiercely debated now as they were one hundred years ago when Old Hickory threw down the gage of battle to Nicholas Biddle.

[NOTE: The statement by Claude G. Bowers on p. viii is quoted from *The Party Battles of the Jackson Period* (Boston, 1922), pp. 318 f., by permission of Houghton Mifflin Company.]

CONTENTS

The Clash of Issues

Jackson's Veto Message:

"It is to be regretted that the rich and powerful too often bend the acts of government to their selfish purposes. . . . In the full enjoyment of the gifts of Heaven and the fruits of superior industry, economy, and virtue, every man is equally entitled to protection by law; but when the laws undertake to add to these natural and just advantages artificial distinctions, to grant titles, gratuities, and exclusive privileges, to make the rich richer and the potent more powerful, the humble members of society — the farmers, mechanics, and laborers — who have neither the time nor the means of securing like favors to themselves, have a right to complain of the injustice of their Government. . . . In the act before me there seems to be a wide and unnecessary departure from . . . just principles."

Daniel Webster, Jackson's political opponent:

"This message . . . manifestly seeks to inflame the poor against the rich; it wantonly attacks whole classes of the people, for the purpose of turning against them the prejudices and the resentments of other classes. It is a state paper which finds no topic too exciting for its use, no passion too inflammable for its address and its solicitation."

Ralph C. H. Catterall, the historian of the Bank:

"Jackson and his supporters committed an offense against the nation when they destroyed the bank. The magnitude and enormity of that offense can only be faintly realized, but one is certainly justified in saying that few greater enormities are chargeable to politicians than the destruction of the Bank of the United States."

Claude G. Bowers, a historian sympathetic to Jackson:

"Even among the ultra-conservatives of business, the feeling was germinating that Jackson was not far wrong in the conclusion that a moneyed institution possessing the power to precipitate panics to influence governmental action, was dangerous to the peace, prosperity, and liberty of the people."

George Rogers Taylor:

A BRIEF HISTORY OF THE SECOND BANK OF THE UNITED STATES

EARLY in January, 1817, the second Bank of the United States opened for business in Carpenter's Hall, Philadelphia. In this building the first Bank of the United States had wound up its affairs six years before. It was appropriate that the second Bank should begin at the old stand, for, although considerably larger, it was organized along lines substantially similar to those of its predecessor. And it was an augury of its future financial power that in 1821 it should move from the modest quarters where the old bank had quietly performed its functions to a sumptuous temple built for its occupancy and designed by William Strickland on lines of the Parthenon in Athens.

Why should the same political party and even many of the same persons who had refused to recharter the Bank of the United States in 1811 have voted to establish an even larger institution in 1816? The chief reason was the war, a war which had been fought on the military front with an inefficiency and ineptness rivaled only in the administration of the government's finances. Congress failed to pass adequate tax laws until the war was nearly over, and the administration of the treasury under William Jones and George W. Campbell proved almost incredibly bad. By the beginning of 1815

the credit of the United States had fallen to its lowest ebb since the founding of the federal government. The war department was pressed to find enough money to pay a bill for $30, and the treasury could not secure funds to meet the interest on that part of the public debt held in New England. Banks had multiplied during the war and greatly extended their note issues. By the fall of 1814 most banks outside New England had been forced to suspend specie payments. The currency consisted of a flood of bank notes circulating at varying discounts and increasing quantities of United States Treasury notes also of fluctuating value. Prices had risen to the highest point for the whole nineteenth century.

As one means of bringing some order out of this chaos and assisting the government in financing the war, sentiment grew for the re-establishment of a national bank. Leaders in promoting this movement were John Jacob Astor, David Parish, Stephen Girard, and other wealthy merchants. Their patriotic sentiments were in happy accord with their personal financial interests. They believed the establishment of a national bank would aid the government to finance the war and would also raise the price of government stock in which they

From the manuscript of Volume 4 of *The Economic History of the United States,* to be published by Rinehart and Company, Inc.

were heavy investors. With their approval President Madison appointed and the Senate confirmed, October, 1814, Alexander Dallas as Secretary of the Treasury. An able Philadelphia lawyer known to favor the establishment of a national bank, he and Senator John C. Calhoun were most active in drawing up plans for a new bank charter. After a great deal of debate and compromise a bill satisfactory to the administration was prepared. President Madison overcame his constitutional scruples and, despite the efforts of Daniel Webster and John Randolph, who led two opposition groups, the act was passed and approved by the President on April 10, 1816.

The charter provided that the capital of the second Bank of the United States should be $35,000,000, of which one fifth was to be subscribed by the federal government. The shareholders were to elect twenty directors of the Bank and the President of the United States was to appoint five. The new institution could issue notes in denominations of not less than $5 which would be accepted by the government in payment for taxes; the total value of notes issued must not exceed $35,000,000. Notes must be redeemed in specie or the Bank was to forfeit twelve per cent per annum on any part of its circulation not so redeemed. The federal government was to receive $1,500,000 from the Bank in return for the charter privilege.

Although earlier proponents had looked upon it mainly as a means for aiding the treasury in financing the war, the chief objects sought by the Bank's sponsors in 1816 were to force the state banks to resume specie payments and to establish a satisfactory national currency. In view of later controversies as to its function it is worth noting that Secretary Dallas regarded it as much more than merely a giant commercial bank. Thus he wrote to Calhoun, December 24, 1815: " . . . it is not an institution created for the purposes of commerce and profit alone, but more for the purposes of national policy, as an auxiliary in the exercise of some of the highest powers of the Government." Nevertheless many, including some government officials and officers of the Bank, did not hold this broad view but appear to have regarded the Bank as merely a great financial institution chiefly obligated to make profits for its stockholders.

Unfortunately, the Bank got off to a bad start and soon headed into serious trouble. President Madison and Secretary Dallas had agreed that the Bank should be under strong Republican influence and succeeded in having William Jones, an ardent Republican politician of Philadelphia, elected as the first president. Why this man who during the war had shown notorious incompetence as Secretary of Navy and Acting Secretary of Treasury should have been chosen for this key position is difficult to understand. Apparently his contemporaries regarded him as a loyal political follower and a trustworthy individual. At any rate he at once adopted a loose, expansionist policy for the Bank, seemingly with the purpose of maximizing profits for stockholders. Branches were promptly opened in the more important commercial cities of the country and loans and discounts rapidly expanded, especially in these branch offices.

Trouble first developed in the branches, which were subjected to little or no control by the parent institution. The Baltimore branch from the beginning was in the hands of a ring of unscrupulous operators who easily robbed it of more than a million dollars before they were exposed and the branch forced into the hands of a receiver. Most of the members of the board of directors of the parent bank speculated in the Bank's own stock, and Jones himself accepted a present of $18,000 which his officers "earned" for him by this kind of speculation. Whether in the branches or in the main office in Philadelphia, wherever one might look, there was malfeasance, misfeasance, or merely administrative incompetence. In January, 1819, President Jones was permitted to resign. In less than two years he had established the greatest financial institution in the country and brought it perilously close to bankruptcy.

The Bank was saved by Langdon Cheves, a respected South Carolina lawyer who became president in 1819 and remained in that position until 1823. Brought in to restore the financial soundness of the institution, he promptly and decisively tightened the administration, for the first time brought the branches under control, sharply reduced the loans outstanding, and began action to collect on the defaulted debts of both state banks and individuals. By 1820 the notes of the Bank in circulation had been reduced to about $3,500,000 from over $8,000,000 in 1818 and loans to $31,401,-000 from $41,181,000. Cheves's methods promptly returned the Bank to financial soundness but his conservative policies resulted in reduced dividends to stockholders, who soon became restive and began to demand more creative leadership. Cheves resigned in the fall of 1823 to be succeeded by Nicholas Biddle, a brilliant, strong-willed man of 37, who had already made a favorable reputation for himself as a writer, as a member of the Pennsylvania senate, and as one of the government directors of the second Bank of the United States.

Long before Biddle took over, the Bank had acquired the bitter hostility of the state banks. In fact, the Bank of the United States could do little which did not evoke the jealousy of these local institutions. When Jones, following a policy of expansion, had established branches in western and southern cities, the local banks had protested against such competition and secured state legislation designed to curtail the operations of the branches. Two states, Indiana (1816) and Illinois (1818), prohibited by provisions in their state constitutions the establishment within their borders of any but state banks. Other states, including Maryland, Tennessee, Georgia, North Carolina, Kentucky, and Ohio, levied taxes upon the branches of the Bank of the United States which would have driven the Bank from the states imposing them had it not been for favorable action by the United States Supreme court. In one of his most famous decisions, *M'Culloch v. Maryland,* Chief Justice Marshall in 1819 declared that the second Bank of the United States was a necessary and proper instrument of the United States government for carrying out its fiscal operations and was therefore constitutional. Moreover, he found the attempt of the state of Maryland to tax the Bank unconstitutional because, said he, if this were permitted then a state might ". . . tax all the means employed by the government, to an excess which would defeat all the ends of government."

When under Cheves the Bank reversed its expansionist policy and called in its loans, the hostility of state banks was even greater than when circulation was being extended. The drastic contraction was accompanied by a wave of failures which meant bankruptcy for many business firms and financial institutions, especially in the West and South. With many of the state banks which survived this debacle the second Bank of the United

States was often on bad terms, chiefly because it reasonably enough insisted that the state banks should not remain for long periods indebted to it for huge sums. Under Jones the branch of the Bank of the United States in Savannah, Georgia, had extended credits of about $200,000 to the state banks of that city. The Bank of the United States under Cheves tried to reduce this debt and made an extremely liberal offer permitting the state banks to use $100,000 without interest if they paid all in excess of that amount. The state banks in rejecting this offer attacked the Bank of the United States as a "mammoth" come to destroy them. Not until the dispute had gone to the Supreme Court was the Bank of the United States able to enforce its claims against the Savannah banks.

Under Biddle the bank soon began cautiously to expand its operations and to assume a position of strength and prosperity. Growth, relatively moderate through 1828, accelerated thereafter. Bank notes issued averaged $4,500,000 in 1823, $11,000,000 in 1828, and $19,000,000 in 1831. Emphasis was placed on commercial loans of short maturity, and transactions in domestic bills of exchange greatly increased. These latter totaled nearly $9,000,000 in 1823, rose to $21,400,000 in 1828, and reached $49,500,000 by 1831. At the same time earnings increased greatly. By 1828 a surplus of $1,500,000 had been accumulated and in the latter half of that year the Bank began paying dividends at the rate of 7 per cent per annum, a rate which it continued as long as it retained its charter.

The operations of the Bank had at last reached a scale sufficient to permit it to perform the dominant role for which it had been originally cast. From the beginning it had proved an efficient fiscal agent for the federal government, not only acting as a safe depository for treasury funds but also successfully transferring these funds from one part of the country to another and meeting government drafts for disbursement at each of its branches. For the years 1816–1827, the Bank transferred funds for the United States Treasury averaging about $28,000,000 per year at a saving estimated at more than $1,000,000. Moreover, the government secured necessary funds quickly and economically from the Bank of the United States whenever borrowing was necessary.

In the second place, the Bank of the United States helped to create a sound national currency both by maintaining specie payments on its own notes and by bringing pressure on the state banks to do the same. During Jones's presidency the Bank had attempted to accept the notes of all its branches at face value whenever they were presented at any of its offices. This could not be continued, for western branches expanded their note issues to meet the need for exchange on the East with the result that the eastern branches accepting these notes were stripped of their specie. The policy was therefore changed to one which honored bank notes at face value in specie only at Philadelphia and at the branch of issue; at a distance from the place of issue notes circulated at a small discount, usually less than one per cent. This discount was much less than it had ordinarily been before the Bank was established, but it nevertheless gave critics of the Bank an opportunity to accuse it of not maintaining a uniform currency.

On February 20, 1817, after the Bank of the United States had been in actual operation only a little over a month, it was able to get the state banks to resume specie payments, and from that time on, assisted by the United States Treasury, it did much to force state banks to remain on a specie-paying basis. However, it must be noted that during much of the period 1818–1822 many of these local institutions were only nominally on a specie basis. Many could not possibly have paid out specie if the Bank of the United States had insisted on their meeting their outstanding obligations to it. As times improved in the late twenties and early thirties most state banks were better able to meet specie demands but even under favorable circumstances their issues typically provided a satisfactory currency for local purposes only. At any distance from the place of issue their notes usually circulated at a considerable discount.

In the third place, the Bank of the United States helped to make credit and currency more abundant in the West and South. To a very considerable extent the Bank of the United States built up its business outside the eastern states on the basis of capital raised in those states. In doing this it aided the frontier areas by helping to provide both the capital and currency needed for their development.

In modern practice the chief function of a central bank is to act as a bankers' bank, guiding its activities not for the purpose of making a profit but so as to forward the public good by discouraging tendencies to over-expansion in the economy and giving prompt relief to banks and business in times of crisis. This central banking function insofar as it was carried out between 1815 and 1824 was chiefly performed not by the Bank of the United States but by the United States Treasury. Before 1819 it was the Treasury which was most vigorous in attempting to restore specie payments and restrict credit expansion. And in the period of severe liquidation which followed, it was again the United States

Treasury, not the Bank of the United States, which through specie deposits went to the aid of hard-pressed state banks and helped them to weather the storm.

After 1823 under the direction of Biddle the Bank of the United States for a time began to assume real leadership as a central bank. In the sharp crisis of 1825 Biddle, seeing trouble coming, placed a restraining influence on credit expansion by the banking community, and during the period of severe liquidation after the bubble burst he wisely expanded loans, thus easing the impact of the crisis on the financial and business community. Again in 1828 he took somewhat similar action to protect the public interest. But in 1832, when he finally acted to check the over-expansion of business at that time, his position was basically changed, for he was then putting a check on an inflationary movement to which the Bank itself had unwisely lent assistance. Later, in 1833–34, Biddle used the tremendous power of the Bank against the general good to force a disastrous contraction on the business community in his effort to win his personal war with President Jackson.

Unwisely, as later events proved, Biddle applied for recharter of the second Bank of the United States in January, 1832, four years before the existing charter expired. He thus threw down the gage of battle to Andrew Jackson in an election year. Congress passed a bill to continue the Bank with little change and President Jackson vetoed it, July 10, 1832. The veto message declared the Bank unconstitutional and condemned it as a device for giving financial advantage and power to a small and irresponsible group of wealthy persons living in eastern cities and even in foreign countries. Biddle threw the whole influence of the Bank against the election of Jackson, who as we know was re-elected by an overwhelming vote.

But this did not end the Bank war. Suspicious of the Bank and vindictive as well, Jackson believed that the government should promptly begin to remove its deposits in the Bank and force it to prepare for the winding up of its affairs. William J. Duane had been made Secretary of the Treasury early in 1833, soon after McLane left that position to head the State Department. When Duane, a stooge for McLane, who was very close to the Bank group, refused to accept the removal policy, Jackson forced his resignation and appointed in his place his attorney general, Roger B. Taney. Taney definitely opposed the Bank; he had been one of the chief drafters of the President's veto message on the bill to recharter. Actually no appreciable shift of existing deposits took place but as new government receipts came in they were simply placed on deposit in state banks.

Nicholas Biddle, no less headstrong than Jackson and still hoping to force the recharter of the Bank, fought back, not scrupling to utilize the full resources of his institution. Believing that only a drastic credit contraction would convince the administration and the country of the folly of permitting the Bank to go out of existence, he began in August, 1833, to curtail credit, and despite growing protests even from favorably disposed business and banking leaders continued the curtailment to September, 1834. To Wil-

liam Appleton, president of the Boston branch of the Bank, he wrote in January, 1834: "Nothing but the evidence of suffering abroad will produce any effect in Congress." And early in the next month he wrote to another correspondent: ". . . all the other Banks and all the merchants may break, but the Bank of the United States shall not break." Biddle succeeded in precipitating a crisis which in 1834 forced discount rates as high as 18 to 36 per cent and brought great distress to the business community. But by this display of power he ruined whatever chances the Bank may have had for recharter. Many business leaders, even those of conservative tendencies, now turned against that institution. Biddle had demonstrated what his enemies had charged: the ability of the Bank to affect the whole course of business of the country and his willingness to use that power to the public detriment and his own personal advantage.

The subsequent history of the Bank is quickly told. Having failed in 1834 to frighten the government into giving it a new charter, the Bank reversed its policy and greatly expanded its operations. On the expiration of its United States charter in 1836 it secured a new one from the state of Pennsylvania and continued in business until October, 1839, when, caught with greatly over-extended loans, it found itself in serious financial straits and forced to suspend specie payments. It never really recovered and was forced into liquidation in 1841.

Andrew Jackson:

VETO MESSAGE, July 10, 1832

THE bill "to modify and continue" the act entitled "An act to incorporate the subscribers to the Bank of the United States" was presented to me on the 4th July instant. Having considered it with the solemn regard to the principles of the Constitution which the day was calculated to inspire, and come to the conclusion that it ought not to become a law, I herewith return it to the Senate, in which it originated, with my objections.

A bank of the United States is in many respects convenient for the Government and useful to the people. Entertaining this opinion, and deeply impressed with the belief that some of the powers and privileges possessed by the existing bank are unauthorized by the Constitution, subversive of the rights of the States, and dangerous to the liberties of the people, I felt it my duty at an early period of my Administration to call the attention of Congress to the practicability of organizing an institution combining all its advantages and obviating these objections. I sincerely regret that in the act before me I can perceive none of those modifications of the bank charter which are necessary, in my opinion, to make it compatible with justice, with sound policy, or with the Constitution of our country.

The present corporate body, denominated the president, directors, and company of the Bank of the United States, will have existed at the time this act is intended to take effect twenty years. It enjoys an exclusive privilege of banking under the authority of the General Government, a monopoly of its favor and support, and, as a necessary consequence, almost a monopoly of the foreign and domestic exchange. The powers, privileges, and favors bestowed upon it in the original charter, by increasing the value of the stock far above its par value, operated as a gratuity of many millions to the stockholders.

An apology may be found for the failure to guard against this result in the consideration that the effect of the original act of incorporation could not be certainly foreseen at the time of its passage. The act before me proposes another gratuity to the holders of the same stock, and in many cases to the same men, of at least seven millions more. This donation finds no apology in any uncertainty as to the effect of the act. On all hands it is conceded that its passage will increase at least 20 or 30 per cent more the market price of the stock, subject to the payment of the annuity of $200,000 per year secured by the act, thus adding in a moment one-fourth to its par value. It is not our own citizens only who are to receive the bounty of our Government. More than eight millions of the stock of this bank

Reprinted from *House Miscellaneous Documents*, 53 Congress, 2 Session, 1893–1894, II, 576–591.

are held by foreigners. By this act the American Republic proposes virtually to make them a present of some millions of dollars. For these gratuities to foreigners and to some of our own opulent citizens the act secures no equivalent whatever. They are the certain gains of the present stockholders under the operation of this act, after making full allowance for the payment of the bonus.

Every monopoly and all exclusive privileges are granted at the expense of the public, which ought to receive a fair equivalent. The many millions which this act proposes to bestow on the stockholders of the existing bank must come directly or indirectly out of the earnings of the American people. It is due to them, therefore, if their Government sell monopolies and exclusive privileges, that they should at least exact for them as much as they are worth in open market. The value of the monopoly in this case may be correctly ascertained. The twenty-eight millions of stock would probably be at an advance of 50 per cent, and command in market at least $42,000,000 subject to the payment of the present bonus. The present value of the monopoly, therefore, is $17,000,000, and this the act proposes to sell for three millions, payable in fifteen annual installments of $200,000 each.

It is not conceivable how the present stockholders can have any claim to the special favor of the Government. The present corporation has enjoyed its monopoly during the period stipulated in the original contract. If we must have such a corporation, why should not the Government sell out the whole stock and thus secure to the people the full market value of the privileges granted? Why should not Congress create and sell twenty-eight millions of stock, incorporating the purchasers with all the powers and privileges secured in this act and putting the premium upon the sales into the Treasury?

But this act does not permit competition in the purchase of this monopoly. It seems to be predicated on the erroneous idea that the present stockholders have a prescriptive right not only to the favor but to the bounty of Government. It appears that more than a fourth part of the stock is held by foreigners and the residue is held by a few hundred of our own citizens, chiefly of the richest class. For their benefit does this act exclude the whole American people from competition in the purchase of this monopoly and dispose of it for many millions less than it is worth. This seems the less excusable because some of our citizens not now stockholders petitioned that the door of competition might be opened, and offered to take a charter on terms much more favorable to the Government and country.

But this proposition, although made by men whose aggregate wealth is believed to be equal to all the private stock in the existing bank, has been set aside, and the bounty of our Government is proposed to be again bestowed on the few who have been fortunate enough to secure the stock and at this moment wield the power of the existing institution. I can not perceive the justice or policy of this course. If our Government must sell monopolies, it would seem to be its duty to take nothing less than their full value, and if gratuities must be made once in fifteen or twenty years let them not be bestowed on the subjects of a foreign government nor upon a designated and favored class of men in our own country. It is but justice and good policy, as far as the nature of the case will admit, to confine our favors to our own fellow-citizens, and let each in his turn enjoy an opportunity to profit by our bounty. In the bearings of the act before me upon these points I find ample reasons why it should not become a law.

It has been urged as an argument in favor of rechartering the present bank that the calling in its loans will produce great embarrassment and distress. The time allowed to close its concerns is ample, and if it has been well managed its pressure will be light, and heavy only in case its management has been bad. If, therefore, it shall produce distress, the fault will be its own, and it would furnish a reason against renewing a power which has been so obviously abused. But will there ever be a time when this reason will be less powerful? To acknowledge its force is to admit that the bank ought to be perpetual, and as a consequence the present stockholders and those inheriting their rights as successors be established a privileged order, clothed both with great political power and enjoying immense pecuniary advantages from their connection with the Government.

The modifications of the existing charter proposed by this act are not such, in my view, as make it consistent with the rights of the States or the liberties of the people. The qualification of the right of the bank to hold real estate, the limitation of its power to establish branches, and the power reserved to Congress to forbid the circulation of small notes are restrictions comparatively of little value or importance. All the objectionable principles of the existing corporation, and most of its odious features, are retained without alleviation.

The fourth section provides "that the notes or bills of the said corporation, although the same be, on the faces thereof, respectively made payable at one place only, shall nevertheless be received by the said corporation at the bank or at any of the offices of discount and deposit thereof if tendered in liquidation or payment of any balance or balances due to said corporation or to such office of discount and deposit from any other incorporated bank." This provision secures to the State banks a legal privilege in the Bank of the United States which is withheld from all private citizens. If a State bank in Philadelphia owe the Bank of the United States and have notes issued by the St. Louis branch, it can pay the debt with those notes, but if a merchant, mechanic, or other private citizen be in like circumstances he can not by law pay his debt with those notes, but must sell them at a discount or send them to St. Louis to be cashed. This boon conceded to the State banks, though not unjust in itself, is most odious because it does not measure out equal justice to the high and the low, the rich and the poor. To the extent of its practical effect it is a bond of union among the banking establishments of the nation, erecting them into an interest separate from that of the people, and its necessary tendency is to unite the Bank of the United States and the State banks in any measure which may be thought conducive to their common interest.

The ninth section of the act recognizes principles of worse tendency than any provision of the present charter.

It enacts that "the cashier of the bank shall annually report to the Secretary of Treasury the names of all stockholders who are not resident citizens of the United States, and on the application of the treasurer of any State shall make out and transmit to such treasurer a list of stockholders residing in or citizens of such State, with the amount of stock owned by each." Although this provision, taken in connection with a decision of the Supreme Court, surrenders, by its silence, the right of the States to tax the banking institutions created by this corporation under the name of branches throughout the Union, it is evidently intended to be construed as a concession of their right to tax that portion of the stock which may be held by their own citizens and residents. In this light, if the act becomes a law, it will be understood by the States, who will probably proceed to levy a tax equal to that paid upon the stock of banks incorporated by themselves. In some States that tax is now 1 per cent, either on the capital or on the shares, and that may be assumed as the amount which all citizen or resident stockholders would be taxed under the operation of this act. As it is only the stock *held* in the States and not that *employed* within them which would be subject to taxation, and as the names of foreign stockholders are not to be reported to the treasurers of the States, it is obvious that the stock held by them will be exempt from this burden. Their annual profits will therefore be 1 per cent more than the citizen stockholders, and as the annual dividends of the bank may be safely estimated at 7 per cent, the stock will be worth 10 or 15 per cent more to foreigners than to citizens of the United States. To appreciate the effects which this state of things will produce, we must take a brief review of the operations and present condition of the Bank of the United States.

By documents submitted to Congress at the present session it appears that on the 1st of January, 1832, of the twenty-eight millions of private stock in the corporation, $8,405,500 were held by foreigners, mostly of Great Britain. The amount of stock held in the nine Western and Southwestern States is $140,200, and in the four Southern States is $5,623,100, and in the Middle and Eastern States is about $13,522,000. The profits of the bank in 1831, as shown in a statement to Congress, were about $3,455,598; of this there accrued in the nine Western States about $1,640,048; in the four Southern States about $352,507, and in the Middle and Eastern States about $1,463,041. As little stock is held in the West, it is obvious that the debt of the people in that section to the bank is principally a debt to the Eastern and foreign stockholders; that the interest they pay upon it is carried into the Eastern States and into Europe, and that it is a burden upon their industry and a drain of their currency, which no country can bear without inconvenience and occasional distress. To meet this burden and equalize the exchange operations of the bank, the amount of specie drawn from those States through its branches within the last two years, as shown by its official reports, was about $6,000,000. More than half a million of this amount does not stop in the Eastern States, but passes on to Europe to pay the dividends of the foreign stockholders. In the principle of taxation recognized by this act the Western States find no adequate compensation for this perpetual burden on their industry and drain of their currency. The branch bank at Mobile made last year $95,140, yet under the provisions of this act the State of Alabama can raise no revenue from these profitable operations, because not a share of the stock is held by any of her citizens. Mississippi and Missouri are in the same condition in relation to the branches at Natchez and St. Louis, and such, in a greater or less degree, is the condition of every Western State. The tendency of the plan of taxation which this act proposes will be to place the whole United States in the same relation to foreign countries which the Western States now bear to the Eastern. When by a tax on resident stockholders the stock of this bank is made worth 10 or 15 per cent more to foreigners than to residents, most of it will inevitably leave the country.

Thus will this provision in its practical effect deprive the Eastern as well as the Southern and Western States of the means of raising a revenue from the extension of business and great profits of this institution. It will make the American people debtors to aliens in nearly the whole amount due to this bank, and send across the Atlantic from two to five millions of specie every year to pay the bank dividends.

In another of its bearings this provision is fraught with danger. Of the twenty-five directors of this bank five are chosen by the Government and twenty by the citizen stockholders. From all voice in these elections the foreign stockholders are excluded by the charter. In proportion, therefore, as the stock is transferred to foreign holders the extent of suffrage in the choice of directors is curtailed. Already is almost a third of the stock in foreign hands and not represented in elections. It is constantly passing out of the country, and this act will accelerate its departure. The entire control of the institution would necessarily fall into the hands of a few citizen stockholders, and the ease with which the object would be accomplished would be a temptation to designing men to secure that control in their own hands by monopolizing the remaining stock. There is danger that a president and directors would then be able to elect themselves from year to year, and without responsibility or control manage the whole concerns of the bank during the existence of its charter. It is easy to conceive that great evils to our country and its institutions might

flow from such a concentration of power in the hands of a few men irresponsible to the people.

Is there no danger to our liberty and independence in a bank that in its nature has so little to bind it to our country? The president of the bank has told us that most of the State banks exist by its forbearance. Should its influence become concentered, as it may under the operation of such an act as this, in the hands of a self-elected directory whose interests are identified with those of the foreign stockholders, will there not be cause to tremble for the purity of our elections in peace and for the independence of our country in war? Their power would be great whenever they might choose to exert it; but if this monopoly were regularly renewed every fifteen or twenty years on terms proposed by themselves, they might seldom in peace put forth their strength to influence elections or control the affairs of the nation. But if any private citizen or public functionary should interpose to curtail its powers or prevent a renewal of its privileges, it can not be doubted that he would be made to feel its influence.

Should the stock of the bank principally pass into the hands of the subjects of a foreign country, and we should unfortunately become involved in a war with that country, what would be our condition? Of the course which would be pursued by a bank almost wholly owned by the subjects of a foreign power, and managed by those whose interests, if not affections, would run in the same direction there can be no doubt. All its operations within would be in aid of the hostile fleets and armies without. Controlling our currency, receiving our public moneys, and holding thousands of our citizens in dependence, it would be more formidable and dangerous than the naval and military power of the enemy.

If we must have a bank with private stockholders, every consideration of sound policy and every impulse of American feeling admonishes that it should be *purely American.* Its stockholders should be composed exclusively of our own citizens, who at least ought to be friendly to our Government and willing to support it in times of difficulty and danger. So abundant is domestic capital that competition in subscribing for the stock of local banks has recently led almost to riots. To a bank exclusively of American stockholders, possessing the powers and privileges granted by this act, subscriptions for $200,000,000 could be readily obtained. Instead of sending abroad the stock of the bank in which the Government must deposit its funds and on which it must rely to sustain its credit in times of emergency, it would rather seem to be expedient to prohibit its sale to aliens under penalty of absolute forfeiture.

It is maintained by the advocates of the bank that its constitutionality in all its features ought to be considered as settled by precedent and by the decision of the Supreme Court. To this conclusion I can not assent. Mere precedent is a dangerous source of authority, and should not be regarded as deciding questions of constitutional power except where the acquiescence of the people and the States can be considered as well settled. So far from this being the case on this subject, an argument against the bank might be based on precedent. One Congress, in 1791, decided in favor of a bank; another, in 1811, decided against it. One Congress, in 1815, decided against a bank; another, in 1816, decided in its favor. Prior to the present Congress, therefore, the precedents drawn

from that source were equal. If we resort to the States, the expressions of legislative, judicial, and executive opinions against the bank have been probably to those in its favor as 4 to 1. There is nothing in precedent, therefore, which, if its authority were admitted, ought to weigh in favor of the act before me.

If the opinion of the Supreme Court covered the whole ground of this act, it ought not to control the coordinate authorities of this Government. The Congress, the Executive, and the Court must each for itself be guided by its own opinion of the Constitution. Each public officer who takes an oath to support the Constitution swears that he will support it as he understands it, and not as it is understood by others. It is as much the duty of the House of Representatives, of the Senate, and of the President to decide upon the constitutionality of any bill or resolution which may be presented to them for passage or approval as it is of the supreme judges when it may be brought before them for judicial decision. The opinion of the judges has no more authority over Congress than the opinion of Congress has over the judges, and on that point the President is independent of both. The authority of the Supreme Court must not, therefore, be permitted to control the Congress or the Executive when acting in their legislative capacities, but to have only such influence as the force of their reasoning may deserve.

But in the case relied upon the Supreme Court have not decided that all the features of this corporation are compatible with the Constitution. It is true that the court have said that the law incorporating the bank is a constitutional exercise of power by Congress; but taking into view the whole opinion of the court and the reasoning by which they have come to that conclusion, I understand them to have decided that inasmuch as a bank is an appropriate means for carrying into effect the enumerating powers of the General Government, therefore the law incorporating it is in accordance with that provision of the Constitution which declares that Congress shall have power "to make all laws which shall be necessary and proper for carrying those powers into execution." Having satisfied themselves that the word *"necessary"* in the Constitution means *"needful," "requisite," "essential," "conducive to,"* and that *"a bank"* is a convenient, a useful, and essential instrument in the prosecution of the Government's "fiscal operations," they conclude that to "use one must be within the discretion of Congress" and that "the act to incorporate the Bank of the United States is a law made in pursuance of the Constitution;" "but," say they, *"where the law is not prohibited and is really calculated to effect any of the objects intrusted to the Government, to undertake here to inquire into the degree of its necessity would be to pass the line which circumscribes the judicial department and to tread on legislative ground."*

The principle here affirmed is that the "degree of its necessity," involving all the details of a banking institution, is a question exclusively for legislative consideration. A bank is constitutional, but it is the province of the Legislature to determine whether this or that particular power, privilege, or exemption is "necessary and proper" to enable the bank to discharge its duties to the Government, and from their decision there is no appeal to the courts of justice. Under the decision of the Supreme Court, therefore, it is the exclusive province of Congress and the President to decide whether the particular features of this

act are *necessary* and *proper* in order to enable the bank to perform conveniently and efficiently the public duties assigned to it as a fiscal agent, and therefore constitutional, or *unnecessary* and *improper,* and therefore unconstitutional.

Without commenting on the general principle affirmed by the Supreme Court, let us examine the details of this act in accordance with the rule of legislative action which they have laid down. It will be found that many of the powers and privileges conferred on it can not be supposed necessary for the purpose for which it is proposed to be created, and are not, therefore, means necessary to attain the end in view, and consequently not justified by the Constitution.

The original act of incorporation, section 21, enacts "that no other bank shall be established by any future law of the United States during the continuance of the corporation hereby created, for which the faith of the United States is hereby pledged: *Provided,* Congress may renew existing charters for banks within the District of Columbia not increasing the capital thereof, and may also establish any other bank or banks in said District with capitals not exceeding in the whole $6,000,000 if they shall deem it expedient." This provision is continued in force by the act before me fifteen years from the 3d of March, 1836.

If Congress possessed the power to establish one bank, they had power to establish more than one if in their opinion two or more banks had been "necessary" to facilitate the execution of the powers delegated to them in the Constitution. If they possessed the power to establish a second bank, it was a power derived from the Constitution to be exercised from time to time, and at any time when the interests of the country or the emergencies of the Government might make it expedient. It was possessed by one Congress as well as another, and by all Congresses alike, and alike at every session. But the Congress of 1816 have taken it away from their successors for twenty years, and the Congress of 1832 proposes to abolish it for fifteen years more. It can not be *"necessary"* or *"proper"* for Congress to barter away or divest themselves of any of the powers vested in them by the Constitution to be exercised for the public good. It is not *"necessary"* to the efficiency of the bank, nor is it *"proper"* in relation to themselves and their successors. They may *properly* use the discretion vested in them, but they may not limit the discretion of their successors. This restriction on themselves and grant of a monopoly to the bank is therefore unconstitutional.

In another point of view this provision is a palpable attempt to amend the Constitution by an act of legislation. The Constitution declares that "the Congress shall have power to exercise exclusive legislation in all cases whatsoever" over the District of Columbia. Its constitutional power, therefore, to establish banks in the District of Columbia and increase their capital at will is unlimited and uncontrollable by any other power than that which gave authority to the Constitution. Yet this act declares that Congress shall *not* increase the capital of existing banks, nor create other banks with capitals exceeding in the whole $6,000,000. The Constitution declares that Congress *shall* have power to exercise exclusive legislation over this District *"in all cases whatsoever,"* and this act declares they shall not. Which is the supreme law of the land? This provision can not be *"necessary"* or *"proper"* or *constitutional* unless the absurdity be admitted that whenever it be "necessary and proper" in the opinion of Congress they have a right to barter away one

portion of the powers vested in them by the Constitution as a means of executing the rest.

On two subjects only does the Constitution recognize in Congress the power to grant exclusive privileges or monopolies. It declares that "Congress shall have power to promote the progress of science and useful arts by securing for limited times to authors and inventors the exclusive right to their respective writings and discoveries." Out of this express delegation of power have grown our laws of patents and copyrights. As the Constitution expressly delegates to Congress the power to grant exclusive privileges in these cases as the means of executing the substantive power "to promote the progress of science and useful arts," it is consistent with the fair rules of construction to conclude that such a power was not intended to be granted as a means of accomplishing any other end. On every other subject which comes within the scope of Congressional power there is an ever-living discretion in the use of proper means, which can not be restricted or abolished without an amendment of the Constitution. Every act of Congress, therefore, which attempts by grants of monopolies or sale of exclusive privileges for a limited time, or a time without limit, to restrict or extinguish its own discretion in the choice of means to execute its delegated powers is equivalent to a legislative amendment of the Constitution, and palpably unconstitutional.

This act authorizes and encourages transfers of its stock to foreigners and grants them an exemption from all State and national taxation. So far from being *"necessary and proper"* that the bank should possess this power to make it a safe and efficient agent of the Government in its fiscal operations, it is calculated to convert the Bank of the United

States into a foreign bank, to impoverish our people in time of peace, to disseminate a foreign influence through every section of the Republic, and in war to endanger our independence.

The several States reserved the power at the formation of the Constitution to regulate and control titles and transfers of real property, and most, if not all, of them have laws disqualifying aliens from acquiring or holding lands within their limits. But this act, in disregard of the undoubted right of the States to prescribe such disqualifications, gives to alien stockholders in this bank an interest and title, as members of the corporation, to all the real property it may acquire within any of the States of this Union. This privilege granted to aliens is not *"necessary"* to enable the bank to perform its public duties, nor in any sense *"proper,"* because it is vitally subversive of the rights of the States.

The Government of the United States have no constitutional power to purchase lands within the States except "for the erection of forts, magazines, arsenals, dockyards, and other needful buildings," and even for these objects only "by the consent of the legislature of the State in which the same shall be." By making themselves stockholders in the bank and granting to the corporation the power to purchase lands for other purposes they assume a power not granted in the Constitution and grant to others what they do not themselves possess. It is not *"necessary"* to the receiving, safe-keeping, or transmission of the funds of the Government that the bank should possess this power, and it is not *"proper"* that Congress should thus enlarge the powers delegated to them in the Constitution.

The old Bank of the United States possessed a capital of only $11,000,000, which was found fully sufficient to enable it with dispatch and safety to perform all the functions required of it by the Government. The capital of the present bank is $35,000,000 — at least twenty-four more than experience has proved to be *necessary* to enable a bank to perform its public functions. The public debt which existed during the period of the old bank and on the establishment of the new has been nearly paid off, and our revenue will soon be reduced. This increase of capital is therefore not for public but for private purposes.

The Government is the only *"proper"* judge where its agents should reside and keep their offices, because it best knows where their presence will be *"necessary."* It can not, therefore, be *"necessary"* or *"proper"* to authorize the bank to locate branches where it pleases to perform the public service, without consulting the Government, and contrary to its will. The principle laid down by the Supreme Court concedes that Congress can not establish a bank for purposes of private speculation and gain, but only as a means of executing the delegated powers of the General Government. By the same principle a branch bank can not constitutionally be established for other than public purposes. The power which this act gives to establish two branches in any State, without the injunction or request of the Government and for other than public purposes, is not *"necessary"* to the due *execution* of the powers delegated to Congress.

The bonus which is exacted from the bank is a confession upon the face of the act that the powers granted by it are greater than are *"necessary"* to its character of a fiscal agent. The Government does not tax its officers and agents for the privilege of serving it. The bonus of a million and a half required by the original charter and that of three millions proposed by this act are not exacted for the privilege of granting "the necessary facilities for transferring the public funds from place to place within the United States or the Territories thereof, and for distributing the same in payment of the public creditors without charging commission or claiming allowance on account of the difference of exchange," as required by the act of incorporation, but for something more beneficial to the stockholders. The original act declares that it (the bonus) is granted "in consideration of the exclusive privileges and benefits conferred by this act upon the said bank," and the act before me declares it to be "in consideration of the exclusive benefits and privileges continued by this act to the said corporation for fifteen years, as aforesaid." It is therefore for "exclusive privileges and benefits" conferred for their own use and emolument, and not for the advantage of the Government, that a bonus is exacted. These surplus powers for which the bank is required to pay can not surely be "*necessary*" to make it the fiscal agent of the Treasury. If they were, the exaction of a bonus for them would not be "*proper.*"

It is maintained by some that the bank is a means of executing the constitutional power "to coin money and regulate the value thereof." Congress have established a mint to coin money and passed laws to regulate the value thereof. The money so coined, with its value so regulated, and such foreign coins as Congress may adopt are the only currency known to the Constitution. But if they have other power to regulate the currency, it was conferred to be exercised by themselves, and not to be transferred to a corporation. If the bank be established for that purpose, with a charter unalterable without its consent, Congress have parted with their power for a term of years, during which the Constitution is a dead

letter. It is neither necessary nor proper to transfer its legislative power to such a bank, and therefore unconstitutional.

By its silence, considered in connection with the decision of the Supreme Court in the case of McCulloch against the State of Maryland, this act takes from the States the power to tax a portion of the banking business carried on within their limits, in subversion of one of the strongest barriers which secured them against Federal encroachments. Banking, like farming, manufacturing, or any other occupation or profession, is *a business*, the right to follow which is not originally derived from the laws. Every citizen and every company of citizens in all of our States possessed the right until the State legislatures deemed it good policy to prohibit private banking by law. If the prohibitory State laws were now repealed, every citizen would again possess the right. The State banks are a qualified restoration of the right which has been taken away by the laws against banking, guarded by such provisions and limitations as in the opinion of the State legislatures the public interest requires. These corporations, unless there be an exemption in their charter, are, like private bankers and banking companies, subject to State taxation. The manner in which these taxes shall be laid depends wholly on legislative discretion. It may be upon the bank, upon the stock, upon the profits, or in any other mode which the sovereign power shall will.

Upon the formation of the Constitution the States guarded their taxing power with peculiar jealousy. They surrendered it only as it regards imports and exports. In relation to every other object within their jurisdiction, whether persons, property, business, or professions, it was secured in as ample a manner as it was before possessed. All persons, though United States officers, are liable to a poll tax by the States within which they reside. The lands of the United States are liable to the usual land tax, except in the new States, from whom agreements that they will not tax unsold lands are exacted when they are admitted into the Union. Horses, wagons, any beasts or vehicles, tools, or property belonging to private citizens, though employed in the service of the United States, are subject to State taxation. Every private business, whether carried on by an officer of the General Government or not, whether it be mixed with public concerns or not, even if it be carried on by the Government of the United States itself, separately or in partnership, falls within the scope of the taxing power of the State. Nothing comes more fully within it than banks and the business of banking, by whomsoever instituted and carried on. Over this whole subject-matter it is just as absolute, unlimited, and uncontrollable as if the Constitution had never been adopted, because in the formation of that instrument it was reserved without qualification.

The principle is conceded that the States can not rightfully tax the operations of the General Government. They can not tax the money of the Government deposited in the State banks, nor the agency of those banks in remitting it; but will any man maintain that their mere selection to perform this public service for the General Government would exempt the State banks and their ordinary business from State taxation? Had the United States, instead of establishing a bank at Philadelphia, employed a private banker to keep and transmit their funds, would it have deprived Pennsylvania of the right to tax his bank and his usual banking operations? It will not be pretended. Upon what principle, then, are

the banking establishments of the Bank of the United States and their usual banking operations to be exempted from taxation? It is not their public agency or the deposits of the Government which the States claim a right to tax, but their banks and their banking powers, instituted and exercised within State jurisdiction for their private emolument—those powers and privileges for which they pay a bonus, and which the States tax in their own banks. The exercise of these powers within a State, no matter by whom or under what authority, whether by private citizens in their original right, by corporate bodies created by the States, by foreigners or the agents of foreign governments located within their limits, forms a legitimate object of State taxation. From this and like sources, from the persons, property, and business that are found residing, located, or carried on under their jurisdiction, must the States, since the surrender of their right to raise a revenue from imports and exports, draw all the money necessary for the support of their governments and the maintenance of their independence. There is no more appropriate subject of taxation than banks, banking, and bank stocks, and none to which the States ought more pertinaciously to cling.

It can not be *necessary* to the character of the bank as a fiscal agent of the Government that its private business should be exempted from that taxation to which all the State banks are liable, nor can I conceive it *"proper"* that the substantive and most essential powers reserved by the States shall be thus attacked and annihilated as a means of executing the powers delegated to the General Government. It may be safely assumed that none of those sages who had an agency in forming or adopting our Constitution ever imagined that any portion of the taxing power of the States not prohibited to them nor delegated to Congress was to be swept away and annihilated as a means of executing certain powers delegated to Congress.

If our power over means is so absolute that the Supreme Court will not call in question the constitutionality of an act of Congress the subject of which "is not prohibited, and is really calculated to effect any of the objects intrusted to the Government," although, as in the case before me, it takes away powers expressly granted to Congress and rights scrupulously reserved to the States, it becomes us to proceed in our legislation with the utmost caution. Though not directly, our own powers and the rights of the States may be indirectly legislated away in the use of means to execute substantive powers. We may not enact that Congress shall not have the power of exclusive legislation over the District of Columbia, but we may pledge the faith of the United States that as a means of executing other powers it shall not be exercised for twenty years or forever. We may not pass an act prohibiting the States to tax the banking business carried on within their limits, but we may, as a means of executing our powers over other objects, place that business in the hands of our agents and then declare it exempt from State taxation in their hands. Thus may our own powers and the rights of the States, which we can not directly curtail or invade, be frittered away and extinguished in the use of means employed by us to execute other powers. That a bank of the United States, competent to all the duties which may be required by the Government, might be so organized as not to infringe on our own delegated powers or the reserved rights of the States I do not entertain a

doubt. Had the Executive been called upon to furnish the project of such an institution, the duty would have been cheerfully performed. In the absence of such a call it was obviously proper that he should confine himself to pointing out those prominent features in the act presented which in his opinion make it incompatible with the Constitution and sound policy. A general discussion will now take place, eliciting new light and settling important principles; and a new Congress, elected in the midst of such discussion, and furnishing an equal representation of the people according to the last census, will bear to the Capitol the verdict of public opinion, and, I doubt not, bring this important question to a satisfactory result.

Under such circumstances the bank comes forward and asks a renewal of its charter for a term of fifteen years upon conditions which not only operate as a gratuity to the stockholders of many millions of dollars, but will sanction any abuses and legalize any encroachments.

Suspicions are entertained and charges are made of gross abuse and violation of its charter. An investigation unwillingly conceded and so restricted in time as necessarily to make it incomplete and unsatisfactory discloses enough to excite suspicion and alarm. In the practices of the principal bank partially unveiled, in the absence of important witnesses, and in numerous charges confidently made and as yet wholly uninvestigated there was enough to induce a majority of the committee of investigation — a committee which was selected from the most able and honorable members of the House of Representatives — to recommend a suspension of further action upon the bill and a prosecution of the inquiry. As the charter had yet four years to run, and as a renewal now was not necessary to the successful prosecution of its business, it was to have been expected that the bank itself, conscious of its purity and proud of its character, would have withdrawn its application for the present, and demanded the severest scrutiny into all its transactions. In their declining to do so there seems to be an additional reason why the functionaries of the Government should proceed with less haste and more caution in the renewal of their monopoly.

The bank is professedly established as an agent of the executive branch of the Government, and its constitutionality is maintained on that ground. Neither upon the propriety of present action nor upon the provisions of this act was the Executive consulted. It has had no opportunity to say that it neither needs nor wants an agent clothed with such powers and favored by such exemptions. There is nothing in its legitimate functions which makes it necessary or proper. Whatever interest or influence, whether public or private, has given birth to this act, it can not be found either in the wishes or necessities of the executive department, by which present action is deemed premature, and the powers conferred upon its agent not only unnecessary, but dangerous to the Government and country.

It is to be regretted that the rich and powerful too often bend the acts of government to their selfish purposes. Distinctions in society will always exist under every just government. Equality of talents, of education, or of wealth can not be produced by human institutions. In the full enjoyment of the gifts of Heaven and the fruits of superior industry, economy, and virtue, every man is equally entitled to protection by law; but when the laws undertake to add to these natural and just advantages artificial distinctions, to grant titles, gratuities, and exclusive privileges, to make the rich richer and the potent more powerful, the humble members of society — the farmers, mechanics, and laborers — who have neither the time nor the means of securing like favors to themselves, have a right to complain of the injustice of their Government. There are no necessary evils in government. Its evils exist only in its abuses. If it would confine itself to equal protection, and, as Heaven does its rains, shower its favors alike on the high and the low, the rich and the poor, it would be an unqualified blessing. In the act before me there seems to be a wide and unnecessary departure from these just principles.

Nor is our Government to be maintained or our Union preserved by invasions of the rights and powers of the several States. In thus attempting to make our General Government strong we make it weak. Its true strength consists in leaving individuals and States as much as possible to themselves — in making itself felt, not in its power, but in its beneficence; not in its control, but in its protection; not in binding the States more closely to the center, but leaving each to move unobstructed in its proper orbit.

Experience should teach us wisdom. Most of the difficulties our Government now encounters and most of the dangers which impend over our Union have sprung from an abandonment of the legitimate objects of Government by our national legislation, and the adoption of such principles as are embodied in this act. Many of our rich men have not been content with equal protection and equal benefits. but have besought us to make them richer by act of Congress. By attempting to gratify their desires we have in the results of our legislation arrayed section against section, interest against interest, and man against man, in a fearful commotion which threatens to shake the foundations of our Union. It is time to pause in our career to review our principles, and if possible revive that devoted patriotism and spirit of compromise which distinguished the sages of the Revolution and the fathers of our Union. If we can not at once, in justice to interests vested under improvident legislation, make our Government what it ought to be, we can at least take a stand against all new grants of monopolies and exclusive privileges, against any prostitution of our Government to the advancement of the few at the expense of the many, and in favor of compromise and gradual reform in our code of laws and system of political economy.

I have now done my duty to my country. If sustained by my fellow-citizens, I shall be grateful and happy; if not, I shall find in the motives which impel me ample grounds for contentment and peace. In the difficulties which surround us and the dangers which threaten our institutions there is cause for neither dismay nor alarm. For relief and deliverance let us firmly rely on that kind Providence which I am sure watches with peculiar care over the destinies of our Republic, and on the intelligence and wisdom of our countrymen. Through *His* abundant goodness and *their* patriotic devotion our liberty and Union will be preserved.

Daniel Webster: REPLY TO JACKSON'S VETO MESSAGE, July 11, 1832

MR. President, no one will deny the high importance of the subject now before us. Congress, after full deliberation and discussion, has passed a bill, by decisive majorities, in both houses, for extending the duration of the Bank of the United States. It has not adopted this measure until its attention had been called to the subject, in three successive annual messages of the President. The bill having been thus passed by both houses, and having been duly presented to the President, instead of signing and approving it, he has returned it with objections. These objections go against the whole substance of the law originally creating the bank. They deny, in effect, that the bank is constitutional; they deny that it is expedient; they deny that it is necessary for the public service.

It is not to be doubted, that the Constitution gives the President the power which he has now exercised; but while the power is admitted, the grounds upon which it has been exerted become fit subjects of examination. The Constitution makes it the duty of Congress, in cases like this, to reconsider the measure which they have passed, to weigh the force of the President's objections to that measure, and to take a new vote upon the question.

Before the Senate proceeds to this second vote, I propose to make some remarks upon those objections. And, in the first place, it is to be observed, that they are such as to extinguish all hope that the present bank, or any bank at all resembling it, or resembling any known similar institution, can ever receive his approbation. He states no terms, no qualifications, no conditions, no modifications, which can reconcile him to the essential provisions of the existing charter. He is against the bank, and against any bank constituted in a manner known either to this or any other country. One advantage, therefore, is certainly obtained by presenting him the bill. It has caused the President's sentiments to be made known. There is no longer any mystery, no longer a contest between hope and fear, or between those prophets who predicted a *veto* and those who foretold an approval. The bill is negatived; the President has assumed the responsibility of putting an end to the bank; and the country must prepare itself to meet that change in its concerns which the expiration of the charter will produce. Mr. President, I will not conceal my opinion that the affairs of the country are approaching an important and dangerous crisis. At the very moment of almost unparalleled general prosperity, there appears an unaccountable disposition to destroy the most useful and most approved institutions of the government.

Part of a speech delivered before the United States Senate. Reprinted from *The Works of Daniel Webster* (Boston, 1853), III, 416–429, 446 f.

Indeed, it seems to be in the midst of all this national happiness that some are found openly to question the advantages of the Constitution itself; and many more ready to embarrass the exercise of its just power, weaken its authority, and undermine its foundations. How far these notions may be carried, it is impossible yet to say. We have before us the practical result of one of them. The bank has fallen, or is to fall.

It is now certain, that, without a change in our public counsels, this bank will not be continued, nor will any other be established, which, according to the general sense and language of mankind, can be entitled to the name. Within three years and nine months from the present moment, the charter of the bank expires; within that period, therefore, it must wind up its concerns. It must call in its debts, withdraw its bills from circulation, and cease from all its ordinary operations. All this is to be done in three years and nine months; because, although there is a provision in the charter rendering it lawful to use the corporate name for two years after the expiration of the charter, yet this is allowed only for the purpose of suits and for the sale of the estate belonging to the bank, and for no other purpose whatever. The whole active business of the bank, its custody of public deposits, its transfer of public moneys, its dealing in exchange, all its loans and discounts, and all its issues of bills for circulation, must cease and determine on or before the third day of March, 1836; and within the same period its debts must be collected, as no new contract can be made with it, as a corporation, for the renewal of loans, or discount of notes or bills, after that time.

The President is of opinion, that this time is long enough to close the concerns of the institution without inconvenience.

His language is, "The time allowed the bank to close its concerns is ample, and if it has been well managed, its pressure will be light, and heavy only in case its management has been bad. If, therefore, it shall produce distress, the fault will be its own." Sir, this is all no more than general statement, without fact or argument to support it. We know what the management of the bank has been, and we know the present state of its affairs. We can judge, therefore, whether it be probable that its capital can be all called in, and the circulation of its bills withdrawn, in three years and nine months, by any discretion or prudence in management, without producing distress. The bank has discounted liberally, in compliance with the wants of the community. The amount due to it on loans and discounts, in certain large divisions of the country, is great; so great, that I do not perceive how any man can believe that it can be paid, within the time now limited, without distress. Let us look at known facts. Thirty millions of the capital of the bank are now out, on loans and discounts, in the States on the Mississippi and its waters; ten millions of which are loaned on the discount of bills of exchange, foreign and domestic, and twenty millions on promissory notes. Now, Sir, how is it possible that this vast amount can be collected in so short a period without suffering, by any management whatever? We are to remember, that, when the collection of this debt begins, at that same time, the existing medium of payment, that is, the circulation of the bills of the bank, will begin also to be restrained and withdrawn; and thus the means of payment must be limited just when the necessity of making payment becomes pressing. The whole debt is to be paid, and within the same time the whole circulation withdrawn.

The local banks, where there are such, will be able to afford little assistance; because they themselves will feel a full share of the pressure. They will not be in a condition to extend their discounts, but, in all probability, obliged to curtail them. Whence, then, are the means to come for paying this debt? and in what medium is payment to be made? If all this may be done with but slight pressure on the community, what course of conduct is to accomplish it? How is it to be done? What other thirty millions are to supply the place of these thirty millions now to be called in? What other circulation or medium of payment is to be adopted in the place of the bills of the bank? The message, following a singular train of argument, which had been used in this house, has a loud lamentation upon the suffering of the Western States on account of their being obliged to pay even interest on this debt. This payment of interest is itself represented as exhausting their means and ruinous to their prosperity. But if the interest cannot be paid without pressure, can both interest and principal be paid in four years without pressure? The truth is, the interest has been paid, is paid, and may continue to be paid, without any pressure at all; because the money borrowed is profitably employed by those who borrow it, and the rate of interest which they pay is at least two per cent. lower than the actual value of money in that part of the country. But to pay the whole principal in less than four years, losing, at the same time, the existing and accustomed means and facilities of payment created by the bank itself, and to do this without extreme embarrassment, without absolute distress, is, in my judgment, impossible. I hesitate not to say, that, as this *veto* travels to the West, it will depreciate the value of the every man's property from the Atlantic States to the capital of Missouri. Its effects will be felt in the price of lands, the great and leading article of Western property, in the price of crops, in the products of labor, in the repression of enterprise, and in embarrassment to every kind of business and occupation. I state this opinion strongly, because I have no doubt of its truth, and am willing its correctness should be judged by the event. Without personal acquaintance with the Western States, I know enough of their condition to be satisfied that what I have predicted must happen. The people of the West are rich, but their riches consist in their immense quantities of excellent land, in the products of these lands, and in their spirit of enterprise. The actual value of money, or rate of interest, with them is high, because their pecuniary capital bears little proportion to their landed interest. At an average rate, money is not worth less than eight per cent. per annum throughout the whole Western country, notwithstanding that it has now a loan or an advance from the bank of thirty millions, at six per cent. To call in this loan, at the rate of eight millions a year, in addition to the interest on the whole, and to take away, at the same time, that circulation which constitutes so great a portion of the medium of payment throughout that whole region, is an operation, which, however wisely conducted, cannot but inflict a blow on the community of tremendous force and frightful consequences. The thing cannot be done without distress, bankruptcy, and ruin, to many. If the President had seen any practical manner in which this change might be effected without producing these consequences, he would have rendered infinite service to the community by pointing it out. But he has pointed out nothing, he has suggested nothing;

he contents himself with saying, without giving any reason, that, if the pressure be heavy, the fault will be the bank's. I hope this is not merely an attempt to forestall opinion, and to throw on the bank the responsibility of those evils which threaten the country, for the sake of removing it from himself.

The responsibility justly lies with him, and there it ought to remain. A great majority of the people are satisfied with the bank as it is, and desirous that it should be continued. They wished no change. The strength of this public sentiment has carried the bill through Congress, against all the influence of the administration, and all the power of organized party. But the President has undertaken, on his own responsibility, to arrest the measure, by refusing his assent to the bill. He is answerable for the consequences, therefore, which necessarily follow the change which the expiration of the bank charter may produce; and if these consequences shall prove disastrous, they can fairly be ascribed to his policy only, and the policy of his administration.

Although, Sir, I have spoken of the effects of this *veto* in the Western country, it has not been because I considered that part of the United States exclusively affected by it. Some of the Atlantic States may feel its consequences, perhaps, as sensibly as those of the West, though not for the same reasons. The concern manifested by Pennsylvania for the renewal of the charter shows her sense of the importance of the bank to her own interest, and that of the nation. That great and enterprising State has entered into an extensive system of internal improvements, which necessarily makes heavy demands on her credit and her resources; and by the sound and acceptable currency which the bank affords, by the sta-

bility which it gives to private credit, and by occasional advances, made in anticipation of her revenues, and in aid of her great objects, she has found herself benefited, doubtless, in no inconsiderable degree. Her legislature has instructed her Senators here to advocate the renewal of the charter at this session. They have obeyed her voice, and yet they have the misfortune to find that, in the judgment of the President, *the measure is unconstitutional, unnecessary, dangerous to liberty, and is, moreover, ill-timed.*

But, Mr. President, it is not the local interest of the West, nor the particular interest of Pennsylvania, or any other State, which has influenced Congress in passing this bill. It has been governed by a wise foresight, and by a desire to avoid embarrassment in the pecuniary concerns of the country, to secure the safe collection and convenient transmission of public moneys, to maintain the circulation of the country, sound and safe as it now happily is, against the possible effects of a wild spirit of speculation. Finding the bank highly useful, Congress has thought fit to provide for its continuance.

As to the *time* of passing this bill, it would seem to be the last thing to be thought of, as a ground of objection, by the President; since, from the date of his first message to the present time, he has never failed to call our attention to the subject with all possible apparent earnestness. So early as December, 1829, in his message to the two houses, he declares, that he "cannot, in justice to the parties interested, too soon present the subject to the deliberate consideration of the legislature, in order to avoid the evils resulting from precipitancy, in a measure involving such important principles and such deep pecuniary interests." Aware of this early invitation given to

Congress to take up the subject, by the President himself, the writer of the message seems to vary the ground of objection, and, instead of complaining that the time of bringing forward this measure was premature, to insist, rather, that, after the report of the committee of the other house, the bank should have withdrawn its application for the present! But that report offers no just ground, surely, for such withdrawal. The subject was before Congress; it was for Congress to decide upon it, with all the light shed by the report; and the question of postponement, having been made in both houses, was lost, by clear majorities, in each. Under such circumstances, it would have been somewhat singular, to say the least, if the bank itself had withdrawn its application. It is indeed known to everybody, that neither the report of the committee, nor any thing contained in that report, was relied on by the opposers of the renewal. If it has been discovered elsewhere, that that report contained matter important in itself, or which should have led to further inquiry, this may be proof of superior sagacity; for certainly no such thing was discerned by either House of Congress.

But, Sir, do we not now see that it was time, and high time, to press this bill, and to send it to the President? Does not the event teach us, that the measure was not brought forward one moment too early? The time had come when the people wished to know the decision of the administration on the question of the bank. Why conceal it, or postpone its declaration? Why, as in regard to the tariff, give out one set of opinions for the North, and another for the South.

An important election is at hand, and the renewal of the bank charter is a pending object of great interest, and some excitement. Should not the opinions of men high in office, and candidates for reëlection, be known, on this, as on other important public questions? Certainly, it is to be hoped that the people of the United States are not yet mere man-worshippers, that they do not choose their rulers without some regard to their political principles, or political opinions. Were they to do this, it would be to subject themselves voluntarily to the evils which the hereditary transmission of power, independent of all personal qualifications, inflicts on other nations. They will judge their public servants by their acts, and continue or withhold their confidence, as they shall think it merited, or as they shall think it forfeited. In every point of view, therefore, the moment had arrived, when it became the duty of Congress to come to a result, in regard to this highly important measure. The interests of the government, the interests of the people, the clear and indisputable voice of public opinion, all called upon Congress to act without further loss of time. It has acted, and its act has been negatived by the President; and this result of the proceedings here places the question, with all its connections and all its incidents, fully before the people.

Before proceeding to the constitutional question, there are some other topics, treated in the message, which ought to be noticed. It commences by an inflamed statement of what it calls the "favor" bestowed upon the original bank by the government, or, indeed, as it is phrased, the "monopoly of its favor and support"; and through the whole message all possible changes are rung on the "gratuity," the "exclusive privileges," and "monopoly," of the bank charter. Now, Sir, the truth is, that the powers conferred on the bank are such, and no others, as are usually conferred on similar institutions.

They constitute no monopoly, although some of them are of necessity, and with propriety, exclusive privileges. "The original act," says the message, "operated as a gratuity of many millions to the stockholders." What fair foundation is there for this remark? The stockholders received their charter, not gratuitously, but for a valuable consideration in money, prescribed by Congress, and actually paid. At some times the stock has been above *par*, at other times below *par*, according to prudence in management, or according to commercial occurrences. But if, by a judicious administration of its affairs, it had kept its stock always above *par*, what pretence would there be, nevertheless, for saying that such augmentation of its value was a "gratuity" from government? The message proceeds to declare, that the present act proposes another donation, another gratuity, to the same men, of at least seven millions more. It seems to me that this is an extraordinary statement, and an extraordinary style of argument, for such a subject and on such an occasion. In the first place, the facts are all assumed; they are taken for true without evidence. There are no proofs that any benefit to that amount will accrue to the stockholders, nor any experience to justify the expectation of it. It rests on random estimates, or mere conjecture. But suppose the continuance of the charter should prove beneficial to the stockholders: do they not pay for it? They give twice as much for a charter of fifteen years, as was given before for one of twenty. And if the proposed *bonus*, or premium, be not, in the President's judgment, large enough, would he, nevertheless, on such a mere matter of opinion as that, negative the whole bill? May not Congress be trusted to decide even on such a subject as the amount of the money premium

to be received by government for a charter of this kind?

But, Sir, there is a larger and a much more just view of this subject. The bill was not passed for the purpose of benefiting the present stockholders. Their benefit, if any, is incidental and collateral. Nor was it passed on any idea that they had a *right* to a renewed charter, although the message argues against such right, as if it had been somewhere set up and asserted. No such right has been asserted by any body. Congress passed the bill, not as a bounty or a favor to the present stockholders, nor to comply with any demand of right on their part; but to promote great public interests, for great public objects. Every bank must have some stockholders, unless it be such a bank as the President has recommended, and in regard to which he seems not likely to find much concurrence of other men's opinions; and if the stockholders, whoever they may be, conduct the affairs of the bank prudently, the expectation is always, of course, that they will make it profitable to themselves, as well as useful to the public. If a bank charter is not to be granted, because, to some extent, it may be profitable to the stockholders, no charter can be granted. The objection lies against all banks.

Sir, the object aimed at by such institutions is to connect the public safety and convenience with private interests. It has been found by experience, that banks are safest under private management, and that government banks are among the most dangerous of all inventions. Now, Sir, the whole drift of the message is to reverse the settled judgment of all the civilized world, and to set up government banks, independent of private interest or private control. For this purpose the message labors, even beyond the measure of all its other labors, to create jealousies and prejudices, on the ground of the alleged benefit which individuals will derive from the renewal of this charter. Much less effort is made to show that government, or the public, will be injured by the bill, than that individuals will profit by it. Following up the impulses of the same spirit, the message goes on gravely to allege, that the act, as passed by Congress, proposes to make a *present* of some millions of dollars to foreigners, because a portion of the stock is held by foreigners. Sir, how would this sort of argument apply to other cases? The President has shown himself not only willing, but anxious, to pay off the three per cent. stock of the United States at *par,* notwithstanding that it is notorious that foreigners are owners of the greater part of it. Why should he not call that a donation to foreigners of many millions?

I will not dwell particularly on this part of the message. Its tone and its arguments are all in the same strain. It speaks of the certain gain of the present stockholders, of the value of the monopoly; it says that all monopolies are granted at the expense of the public; that the many millions which this bill bestows on the stockholders come out of the earnings of the people; that, if government sells monopolies, it ought to sell them in open market; that it is an erroneous idea, that the present stockholders have a prescriptive right either to the favor or the bounty of government; that the stock is in the hands of a few, and that the whole American people are excluded from competition in the purchase of the monopoly. To all this I say, again, that much of it is assumption without proof; much of it is an argument against that which nobody has maintained or asserted; and the rest of it would be equally strong against

any charter, at any time. These objections existed in their full strength, whatever that was, against the first bank. They existed, in like manner, against the present bank at its creation, and will always exist against all banks. Indeed, all the fault found with the bill now before us is, that it proposes to continue the bank substantially as it now exists. "All the objectionable principles of the existing corporation," says the message, "and most of its odious features, are retained without alleviation"; so that the message is aimed against the bank, as it has existed from the first, and against any and all others resembling it in its general features.

Allow me, now, Sir, to take notice of an argument founded on the practical operation of the bank. That argument is this. Little of the stock of the bank is held in the West, the capital being chiefly owned by citizens of the Southern and Eastern States, and by foreigners. But the Western and Southwestern States owe the bank a heavy debt, so heavy that the interest amounts to a million six hundred thousand a year. This interest is carried to the Eastern States, or to Europe, annually, and its payment is a burden on the people of the West, and a drain of their currency, which no country can bear without inconvenience and distress. The true character and the whole value of this argument are manifest by the mere statement of it. The people of the West are, from their situation, necessarily large borrowers. They need money, capital, and they borrow it, because they can derive a benefit from its use, much beyond the interest which they pay. They borrow at six per cent. of the bank, although the value of money with them is at least as high as eight. Nevertheless, although they borrow at this low rate of interest, and although they use all they borrow thus profitably, yet they cannot pay the interest without "inconvenience and distress"; and then, Sir, follows the logical conclusion, that, although they cannot pay even the interest without inconvenience and distress, yet less than four years is ample time for the bank to call in the whole, both principal and interest, without causing more than a light pressure. This is the argument.

Then follows another, which may be thus stated. It is competent to the States to tax the property of their citizens vested in the stock of this bank; but the power is denied of taxing the stock of foreigners; therefore the stock will be worth ten or fifteen per cent more to foreigners than to residents, and will of course inevitably leave the country, and make the American people debtors to aliens in nearly the whole amount due the bank, and send across the Atlantic from two to five millions of specie every year, to pay the bank dividends.

Mr. President, arguments like these might be more readily disposed of, were it not that the high and official source from which they proceed imposes the necessity of treating them with respect. In the first place, it may safely be denied that the stock of the bank is any more valuable to foreigners than to our own citizens, or an object of greater desire to them, except in so far as capital may be more abundant in the foreign country, and therefore its owners more in want of opportunity of investment. The foreign stockholder enjoys no exemption from taxation. He is, of course, taxed by his own government for his incomes, derived from this as well as other property; and this is a full answer to the whole statement. But it may be added, in the second place, that it is not the practice of civilized states to tax the property of foreigners under such circumstances. Do

we tax, or did we ever tax, the foreign holders of our public debt? Does Pennsylvania, New York, or Ohio tax the foreign holders of stock in the loans contracted by either of these States? Certainly not. Sir, I must confess I had little expected to see, on such an occasion as the present, a labored and repeated attempt to produce an impression on the public opinion unfavorable to the bank, from the circumstance that foreigners are among its stockholders. I have no hesitation in saying, that I deem such a train of remark as the message contains on this point, coming from the President of the United States, to be injurious to the credit and character of the country abroad; because it manifests a jealousy, a lurking disposition not to respect the property, of foreigners invited hither by our own laws. And, Sir, what is its tendency but to excite this jealousy, and create groundless prejudices?

From the commencement of the government, it has been thought desirable to invite, rather than to repel, the introduction of foreign capital. Our stocks have all been open to foreign subscriptions; and the State banks, in like manner, are free to foreign ownership. Whatever State has created a debt has been willing that foreigners should become purchasers, and desirous of it. How long is it, Sir, since Congress itself passed a law vesting new powers in the President of the United States over the cities in this District, for the very purpose of increasing their credit abroad, the better to enable them to borrow money to pay their subscriptions to the Chesapeake and Ohio Canal? It is easy to say that there is danger to liberty, danger to independence, in a bank open to foreign stockholders, because it is easy to say any thing. But neither reason nor experience proves any such danger. The foreign stockholder cannot be a director. He has no voice even in the choice of directors. His money is placed entirely in the management of the directors appointed by the President and Senate and by the American stockholders. So far as there is dependence or influence either way, it is to the disadvantage of the foreign stockholder. He has parted with the control over his own property, instead of exercising control over the property or over the actions of others. And, Sir, let it now be added, in further answer to this class of objections, that experience has abundantly confuted them all. This government has existed forty-three years, and has maintained, in full being and operation, a bank, such as is now proposed to be renewed, for thirty-six years out of the forty-three. We have never for a moment had a bank not subject to every one of these objections. Always, foreigners might be stockholders; always, foreign stock has been exempt from State taxation, as much as at present; always the same power and privileges; always, all that which is now called a "monopoly," a "gratuity," a "present," has been possessed by the bank. And yet there has been found no danger to liberty, no introduction of foreign influence, and no accumulation of irresponsible power in a few hands. I cannot but hope, therefore, that the people of the United States will not now yield up their judgment to those notions which would reverse all our best experience, and persuade us to discontinue a useful institution from the influence of vague and unfounded declamation against its danger to the public liberties. Our liberties, indeed, must stand upon very frail foundations, if the government cannot, without endangering them, avail itself of those common facilities, in the collection of its revenues and the management of its finances, which

all other governments, in commercial countries, find useful and necessary.

In order to justify its alarm for the security of our independence, the message supposes a case. It supposes that the bank should pass principally into the hands of the subjects of a foreign country, and that we should be involved in war with that country, and then it exclaims, "What would be our condition?" Why, Sir, it is plain that all the advantages would be on our side. The bank would still be our institution, subject to our own laws, and all its directors elected by ourselves; and our means would be enhanced, not by the confiscation and plunder, but by the proper use, of the foreign capital in our hands. And, Sir, it is singular enough, that this very state of war, from which this argument against a bank is drawn, is the very thing which, more than all others, convinced the country and the government of the necessity of a national bank. So much was the want of such an institution felt in the late war, that the subject engaged the attention of Congress, constantly, from the declaration of that war down to the time when the existing bank was actually established; so that in this respect, as well as in others, the argument of the message is directly opposed to the whole experience of the government, and to the general and long-settled convictions of the country. . . .

Mr. President, we have arrived at a new epoch. We are entering on experiments, with the government and the Constitution of the country, hitherto untried, and of fearful and appalling aspect. This message calls us to the contemplation of a future which little resembles the past. Its principles are at war with all that public opinion has sustained, and all which the experience of the government has sanctioned. It denies first principles;

it contradicts truths, heretofore received as indisputable. It denies to the judiciary the interpretation of law, and claims to divide with Congress the power of originating statutes. It extends the grasp of executive pretension over every power of the government. But this is not all. It presents the chief magistrate of the Union in the attitude of arguing away the powers of that government over which he has been chosen to preside; and adopting for this purpose modes of reasoning which, even under the influence of all proper feeling towards high official station, it is difficult to regard as respectable. It appeals to every prejudice which may betray men into a mistaken view of their own interests, and to every passion which may lead them to disobey the impulses of their understanding. It urges all the specious topics of State rights and national encroachment against that which a great majority of the States have affirmed to be rightful, and in which all of them have acquiesced. It sows, in an unsparing manner, the seeds of jealousy and ill-will against that government of which its author is the official head. It

raises a cry, that liberty is in danger, at the very moment when it puts forth claims to powers heretofore unknown and unheard of. It effects alarm for the public freedom, when nothing endangers that freedom so much as its own unparalleled pretences. This, even, is not all. It manifestly seeks to inflame the poor against the rich; it wantonly attacks whole classes of the people, for the purpose of turning against them the prejudices and the resentments of other classes. It is a state paper which finds no topic too exciting for its use, no passion too inflammable for its address and its solicitation.

Such is this message. It remains now for the people of the United States to choose between the principles here avowed and their government. These cannot subsist together. The one or the other must be rejected. If the sentiments of the message shall receive general approbation, the Constitution will have perished even earlier than the moment which its enemies originally allowed for the termination of its existence. It will not have survived to its fiftieth year.

Boston Daily Atlas: AN EDITORIAL

THE Bank Veto. — This is the most wholly *radical* and basely *Jesuitical* document that ever emanated from any Administration, in any country. It violates all our established notions and feelings. It arraigns Congress for not asking permission of the Executive before daring to legislate on the matter, and fairly intimates a design to save the two houses in future from all such trouble. It impudently asserts that Congress have acted prematurely, blindly, and without sufficient examination. It falsely and wickedly alleges that the rich and powerful throughout the country are waging a war of *oppression* against the poor and the weak; and attempts to justify the President on the ground of its being his duty thus to protect the humble when so assailed. Finally, it unblushingly denies that the Supreme Court is the proper tribunal to decide upon the constitutionality of the laws!!

The whole paper is a most thoroughgoing *electioneering* missile, intended to secure the mad-caps of the South, and as such, deserves the execration of all who love their country or its welfare. *This veto* seems to be the production of the whole *kitchen* cabinet — of hypocrisy and arrogance; of imbecility and talent; of cunning, falsehood, and corruption — a very firebrand, intended to destroy their opponents, but which now, thanks to Him who can bring good out of evil, bids fair to light up a flame that shall consume its vile authors.

If the doctrines avowed in this document do not arouse the Nation, we shall despair that any thing will, until the iron hand of despotism has swept our fair land, and this glorious Republic, if not wholly annihilated, shall have been fiercely shaken to its very foundations.

Reprinted in the *National Intelligencer*, Washington, D. C., August 9, 1832 (Vol. 33, no. 4793), p. 2.

Portland Daily Advertiser: AN EDITORIAL

THERE is no part of the Veto Message more deservedly reprobated, and more reprehensible, than that part which attempts to array the poor against the rich, and thus to set in opposition the prejudices which one class may have against another. The object of all banks, it is more than insinuated, is to make the rich richer and the poor poorer. We will not dwell upon the refutation of so unworthy an insinuation. But we ask the property-holders, if they are willing to lend a hand for some new Agrarian project, which shall upset all the rights of property, and establish an equal division of estates and chattels. A more deranging, radical, law upsetting document was never promulgated by the wildest Roman fanatic. The revolutionists of France went but little further. But how undignified, how disreputable is it, in the President of a constitutional republic to lay his blows not only upon the laws and upon the Judiciary, but even to degrade his station by insinuations, which would do discredit to Cromwell or the *people-loving* Robespierre. Is the President preparing for a crown by cajoling us with the prospect of an equal division of goods — by offering his aid to overturn the rights of property, to humble the wealthy, and to put down the exalted? If so, we ask, which is worth the most, monarchy, despotism, the tyranny of one man — or, honorable poverty, and the present enjoyment of a constitution and laws which throw the field of exertion wide open to industry, energy, and economy? Let it be remembered that every military chieftain, Sylla, Caesar, Cromwell, all have obtained unlimited and despotic power by pretending to be the sole friends of the People and often by denouncing the rich, and by cajoling the poor with prospects, which they never intended to be realized, or only realized with chains and slavery, and dungeons, or enrollment in the legions assembled to add to the power of the tyrant.

Reprinted in the *National Intelligencer*, Washington, D. C., August 9, 1832 (Vol. 33, no. 4793), p. 2.

George Bancroft: A LETTER, Dated Northampton, October 1, 1834

THE United States Bank, as at present constituted, ought never to be renewed. The reasons are obvious.

1. The capital is too vast. In proportion to the wealth of the country, it is the largest moneyed monopoly in the world. Not England with its hundred millions of subjects, and its aristocratic factions for leaders, not the France of Napoleon, nor the legitimacy, nor of Louis Philippe, not Russia with its despotic government and its millions of serfs, has ever created a moneyed institution with resources comparatively so great. Republican America, the Virgin of the New World, the Government which is especially charged by wholesome legislation to prevent all extreme inequalities of fortune, has surpassed every country in Europe in the lavish concession of influence and privileges to a moneyed corporation.

2. There is equal room for objection to the power of the United States Bank to accumulate and retain real estate under the form of mortgages; a power as durable as its charter, equal to that of the Massachusetts General Hospital in its character, and co-extensive with the Union; a feature in the bank, so offensive, that it is now condemned even by its friends.

3. The power of establishing branches at its will in any portion of the Union, is another too lavish concession. An institution, lifted above the local laws, and defying the powers of state legislation, by which it can never be taxed, can offer no just motive for a branch, except where it may be required as an organ of the treasury.

4. The power of the bank to supply the currency with bills of a small denomination, is, in a national point of view, too little restricted. Under its operation and the rivalry of the state banks, specie is almost entirely withdrawn from the hands of the people; and credit, which is so fluctuating and so delicate, has been pushed to such an excess, that every little scarcity in the money market is felt throughout the country with fourfold severity. The excessive use of credit and frequent ruinous pressures are inseparable.

5. The power of the bank to resist inquiry is too great. I hold to the republican doctrine of strict accountability. Every organ of the government, and every corporation that lives by the favor of the government, should be exposed to the searching influence of a "roving hunt" and a diligent inquiry. The severer the scrutiny, the better. . . .

Of these objectives against the United States Bank, the one, relating to its immense capital, is the most weighty. I have been surprised at the apathy of the people on this subject. . . . [We must try to] sink deep in the hearts of the people

This selection is part of a letter addressed to Messrs. S. Judd, J. H. Flint, S. Parsons, C. Clark, C. P. Huntington, and J. Wright, printed in the *Boston Courier*, October 23, 1834.

the conviction, that vast associations of wealth are never to be tolerated. No matter what are the details of the grant, these immense moneyed combinations, whether they present themselves in the shape of a Life and Trust company, with power vast enough to convert the yeomanry of whole countries into a dependant tenantry, or a mammoth State Bank of many millions, or a United States Bank with a capital disproportioned to the wealth and industry of the country, should always be resisted.

The evils of these associations of boundless wealth are of the most deadly kind.

A Bank of thirty-five millions, under a charter like that of the existing bank, may attain an immense political influence, present in every part of the union, blindly following the impulse of one mind, and reckless of consequences in zeal of political ambition. Next to the national executive, the direction of the United States Bank is the most powerful body in the republic. Let the farmers of Massachusetts attempt by a healthful combination to produce an impression on the public mind, and they will learn from the experiment, how feeble and disjoined and ill-continued are their efforts in comparison with that of an association, which controls all the credit that can rest on a capital of thirty-five millions. The gross revenues of the bank may easily be made to amount to five millions of dollars, the net revenue to more than two and a half millions. The state of Massachusetts is also a corporation, with a revenue less than one twelfth part of the actual revenue of the United States Bank. The patronage of the government of Massachusetts is hardly fifty thousand dollars, the patronage of the direction of the United States Bank is between one and two millions, besides the very great

influence which comes from the loan of sixty or seventy millions.

Another and a powerful reason against so great a capital, lies in the control of commercial operations, which is thus secured to a single company, and exercised by a single mind; an objection which would apply with still greater force to any bank; to be managed by the executive or its subservient instruments. No man or body of men ought ever to be invested with such exorbitant powers that, in case of misdemeanor, the guilty cannot be arraigned without plunging the country in distress. . . .

But the great objection in my mind to the continuance of the present United States Bank, lies in its tendency to promote extreme inequalities in point of fortune. It forms a part of a system of deadly hostility to the policy which the country should pursue. The Bank is possessed of immense resources and commanding influence; its sympathies, its prejudices, are all on the side of wealth; and its existence has a steady and evident tendency to conciliate for capital a controlling influence on legislation.

Of all political heresies the most baleful is that, which would base political power on wealth. It is too late to invent theories on the subject; history has solved the question. Where the people possess no authority, their rights obtain no respect. Their political degradation is followed by insult and misery; and the gulf between the rich man and Lazarus perpetually grows wider and deeper. . . . [Examples are cited from Roman, English, and French history.] Show me one instance where popular institutions have violated the rights of property, and I will show you a hundred, nay a thousand instances, where the people have been pillaged by the greedy cupidity of a privileged class. There is more danger from monopolies than from combinations of workmen. There is more danger that capital will swallow up the profits of labor, than that labor will confiscate capital.

Political influence is steadily tending to the summit level of property; and this political influence of wealth must be balanced by the political power of numbers. Even then this political influence often controls elections, and often with a giant's tread, stalks into the halls of legislation.

When the merchant demands that his interests should prevail over those of liberty, it is the clamor of capital. The flag of the United States should protect every bale of goods over which it waves, and carry its guardian influence even to the Falkland Islands or the harbors of Sumatra; to the Antipodes or the Poles; but the control of legislation is too sacred a trust to be surrendered. We tolerate no commercial aristocracy like that of Tyre or Florence, of Carthage or Venice. Here merchants are never to be princes.

When a life and trust company ask for privileges, which enable capital to consume the moderate profits of the farmer by tempting him to incur the hazards of debt, it is the clamor of capital, deafening the voice of benevolence and legislative wisdom.

When the creditor demands that the debtor may once more be allowed to pledge his body and his personal freedom, it is the clamor of capital.

When "vested rights" claim a veto on legislation, and assert themselves as the law paramount in defiance of the consti-tution which makes the common good the supreme rule, it is the clamor of capital, desiring to renew one of the abuses of feudal institutions.

When the usurer invokes the aid of society to enforce the contracts, which he has wrung without mercy from the feverish hopes of pressing necessity, it is the clamor of capital, which like the grave, never says, It is enough.

When employers combine to reduce the wages of labor, and at the same time threaten an indictment for conspiracy against the combinations of workmen, it is the clamor of capital.

The feud between the capitalist and the laborer, the house of Have and the house of Want, is as old as social union, and can never be entirely quieted; but he who will act with moderation, prefer facts to theories, and remember that every thing in this world is relative and not absolute, will see that the violence of the contest may be stilled, if the unreasonable demands of personal interests are subjected to the decisions of even-handed justice. . . .

National happiness is not always increased by the increase of national wealth; a state may be excessively opulent, and its people be wretched, the influence of wealth on happiness depends on the mode of its acquisition and the mode of its distribution. But labor, as it has just been defined, is always a source of happiness. Its object is always good; its healthy abundance is the most cheering spectacle that civilization can offer. Labor should enjoy the happiness which it creates. . . .

Ralph C. H. Catterall:

THE CHARGES AGAINST THE BANK

THE subject in connection with the bank which always arouses most interest is its alleged corrupt connection with politics. It may be said at once that there never has been any evidence produced to show that the bank as a national bank ever spent a dollar corruptly. Yet the accusation was repeated so often that historians have been inclined to accept as proved what was only vehemently asserted, and it begot an incurable suspicion which has endured to this day.

It is self-evident that the bank would be affected by political considerations, since from the beginning to the end of its existence it was to a large extent subject to the will and whim of politicians, and it was frequently attacked by them. Had the board of directors been composed exclusively of canonized saints, still the conciliation of politicians and political forces would have been necessary. The only question worthy of discussion is that of the bank's honesty or corruption in this situation.

Biddle in 1829 rejected as totally inadmissible any attempt to create boards on which the political parties were fairly balanced, and declared that political affiliations should not be considered in such selections. He was right in this; but it must not be supposed that the proposition of a political balance was novel, or

that Jackson Democrats first suggested it, or that there was any moral obliquity in such an arrangement. When the first government directors were named, President Madison frankly selected them all from his own political party, and the private stockholders, quite certain that the bank must either be a political machine or possess a balance of parties, elected ten Republicans and ten Federalists as their members of the board. Madison and his capable and honest secretary, A. J. Dallas, then struggled successfully to secure the presidency of the bank for a Republican partisan of no particular ability or experience as a banker, and thus the disasters consequent upon the presidency of William Jones are primarily chargeable to James Madison and Alexander James Dallas.

The policy of political balance then inaugurated was religiously pursued all through the administration of William Jones, and certainly through part of that of Langdon Cheves. Writing to Biddle in 1820, John McKim urges him to assist in the election of a Republican director at Baltimore, "as you know that the Republicans are one short of their number, and the necessity of giving us our share of the Directors, as we do hold more than the half of the stock, and it having been Policy to divide the two Partys in the direction, since the Bank was established." When this equal division ceased it is not possible to say, but it may be reasonably presumed that the disintegration of parties under Monroe caused its cessation.

Biddle was opposed to the practice, and fought against it strenuously when it was suggested in the case of the Kentucky branches and the branch in New Hampshire in 1829. He then stated that he considered such an arrangement as largely responsible for the bank's losses in the West in the early years of its career. As to his rumored desire to have the bank anti-Jackson, he repudiated it altogether, and constantly wondered why anyone could suppose that a bank would care which political party was up or which was down. He was never weary of quoting Dean Swift's remark that "money is neither Whig nor Tory," and in asserting that "men will lend where they are sure of getting back their money with a profit." This was sound sense, and holding these opinions with deep conviction Biddle was anxious above all to exclude political considerations.

Nevertheless he was not able to carry out his wishes altogether. During Adams's administration members of the party in power were no less ready to complain and to demand assistance from the bank than were the Jackson politicians later. Biddle repulsed them with as little ceremony as he repulsed Ingham, yet he was compelled to consider political affiliations in the appointments to the boards all through his presidency. In January, 1824, there was dissatisfaction in Boston with the political complexion of the directorate there, and B. W. Crowninshield was substituted for a Federalist on the parent board in order to give the other party a chance and to assuage "feelings which may hereafter grow into hostility."

Again in 1828 he retained the services of C. P. White at New York because it was not expedient to "alienate a member of the Board at such a time — to offend personally a member of that Congress before whom the Bank may probably come for a renewal of its charter," while in November, 1832, he was anxious "to conciliate gentlemen who may be useful to the institution."

It will be observed, however, that there was no plan of a political balance in these instances. Another conclusion must also be drawn, that, so far from trying to constitute his boards all of one political party, as the Jackson politicians asserted, Biddle took unusual pains to appoint members of the various parties when he could secure those who were qualified for the positions. After the correspondence with Ingham and the reiterated charges of doing precisely what he wished to avoid, Biddle introduced additional Jackson politicians into the boards. He did this at Baltimore, at New York, at New Orleans, at Portsmouth, at Nashville, at Lexington, and at Utica. He allowed Lewis to name most of the members of the Nashville board, took his advice about the Lexington branch, and ceased his complacency only when he saw reason to suspect that the wily major would soon be naming all the western directorates. In August Lewis wrote saying that he was half ashamed to ask for further favors, but that "Our friends at Louisville, Kentucky, think they are not fairly and equally represented in your Branch at that place," and he forwarded the names of three gentlemen whose appointment would probably "give entire satisfaction to the friends of the administration in that part of the state." This further encroachment upon the province of the bank exhausted the patience of its much-enduring head, and he politely declined to introduce "new members . . . for the purpose of making any political balance." The refusal is creditable to Biddle; it proves that he would not be subservient to the administration even at a most critical moment in the bank's attempts to secure Jackson's assent to a recharter, and that he was fixed in his determination that the bank should not degenerate into a political machine.

It may be argued, however, that while the parent board was free from political chicane and bias, the local boards were not. Such arguments are undoubtedly applicable to the early years of the bank, because in the southern and western states campaigns at times revolved about banking questions and would involve the institution despite itself. Every officer and employee of the Bank of the United States must have been on one side during the struggle between the new and the old court parties in Kentucky, and such occurrences would lead to the conviction that the bank spent money for the purpose of controlling elections which were vital to its interests. It is also certain that a board of directors composed of intelligent business men would contain few members of the Jackson Democracy — a condition which would incur suspicion of political favoritism. As the bank's loans would be made mostly to the same class as that from which the directors were selected, a charge of discriminating against Democrats would inevitably arise.

Consequently assertions of corruption at the branches were frequently made. As early as 1825 it was insinuated that the president of the Washington branch, though recognized as incompetent, had retained possession of his office because of his influence with the Monroe administration. In regard to Kentucky frequent charges of unjustifiable political activity

were made. Blair asserts of his own knowledge that "bank men" employed bribes to influence the elections, though the phrase "bank men" is scarcely sufficient to include officers of the bank. Like assertions were made in reference to Louisiana. From South Carolina reports came of officials of the branch engaging actively in politics. Hill, of New Hampshire, declared in the Senate that the Portsmouth office "was made a party engine" in 1828, and that "it was the principal instrument" in carrying the state for Adams; while Clayton, of Georgia, asserted that the president of the Norfolk branch had engaged most offensively in politics, publicly declaring that he was "opposed to General Jackson," and becoming involved in fisticuffs as a result.

These are the specific charges of political action which admit of examination. The charge against the president of the Washington office is of no moment. He did indeed exert his supposed influence with the administration to secure his election to the local board, and was severely censured for doing so by the president of the bank. In the New Hampshire case no political acts were adduced, and the only circumstances which gave color to the assertions were that the president there was an old-time Federalist and a friend of Webster. The New Orleans charges were admitted by President Jackson to be baseless; those in regard to South Carolina were of a different character. It was asserted that the president there, who was an active politician, had been seen "superintending . . . the polls at the elections" — which might well be without involving the branch. Unfortunately, this officer insisted on taking an active part in the heated campaign over nullification — opposing that heresy with all his power. Biddle wrote him a letter requesting that he refrain from such action, as it was calculated to injure the bank, and added, "no principle is more fundamental than its total abstinence from politics." Johnson's subsequent activity, however, occasioned complaint on the part of Vice-President Calhoun and Senator Hayne. The charge against the Norfolk officer is of the same character. He was at the polls and opposed to General Jackson, but how this involved the bank it is difficult to see. In regard to the charges against the Kentucky branches, Jackson expressed himself as satisfied that they were without foundation as far as the parent board was concerned. The directors there denied them; while Biddle urged the officers to exercise care in avoiding all cause for such complaints.

The actual status of Biddle's policy never showed better than in 1831, when the charges against the Kentucky offices were renewed. Writing to him in April, the cashier of the Lexington office urges loans to help the anti-Jackson candidate, because funds were needed "to win for our men." The president of the branch thought they ought to be furnished, and "so does Mr. Clay. The coming election of Congressmen is all important in its bearing on the Presidential election." To this Biddle instantly and decisively replied: "I believe it to be a fundamental principle in the administration of the Bank that its officers should abstain from any connexion with what are called politics, to abstain not in appearance merely, but entirely, candidly and honestly." Thus at the moment that Blair was charging political corruption in Kentucky, Biddle refused assistance which even Henry Clay thought should be granted. Similarly in 1832, after the veto, Biddle declared that the bank would take no active part in the campaign, such

action being contrary to its principles. To this resolution he adhered.

Unquestionably the bank lobbied in its own interests. It did this in the New York legislature in February and March, 1831, to hinder the adoption of resolutions hostile to it. At the same time it strove to get through the Pennsylvania legislature a resolution in its favor, C. J. Ingersoll acting as its champion. Again, during the struggle for re-charter, Horace Binney acted as its manager at Washington, while in 1834 the bank used its influence with its friends to elect John Sergeant senator from Pennsylvania. The attempt failed, but prevented Richard Rush's election. In all these cases, however, there is no reason to suspect the use of corrupt means; while the suspicion that it used such means to secure re-charter in 1832 is absolutely baseless so far as all the known evidence goes.

What the bank did not do directly, it was frequently charged with doing indirectly. Its enemies declared, with emphatic repetition, that it secured the favor of congressmen and politicians by granting them unusual accommodations on insufficient security and extending to them favors not granted to other individuals. It must be admitted that the bank was accustomed to give drafts for the salaries of congressmen, payable at points distant from Washington, without charging exchange. Biddle said he knew of no such cases, but if they occurred they were defensible on the ground that congressmen had a right to their pay wherever "the Treasury chooses to give it to them." This answer could hardly be considered satisfactory, and the assertion was frequently made that not only did congressmen receive their pay wherever they chose to demand it, thus getting the benefit of the exchange, but that in other instances they were accommodated without being charged exchange. Such a practice was certainly open to the objection of being in the nature of granting favors to those from whom favors were to be expected. The same condemnation must fall upon the practice of paying congressmen and government officials before their salaries became due by the passage of the general appropriations act. Adams, a warm champion of the bank, showed that in a single session the amount thus advanced was almost $400,000, "which was equivalent to a loan without interest," and that the amount of interest thus lost to the bank was over $3,000. He was "not without doubts of the propriety of this indulgence."

That congressmen were not to borrow money, or that the bank was not to lend them money, could hardly be argued, since this would be an unwarrantable discrimination against congressmen as congressmen. That the officers of the bank were willing to make loans on easy terms to congressmen is likely, and is illustrated in the case of General Stevens, to whom Biddle granted a loan on his own authority, although he was a stranger, and although the president did not know that the drawers of the notes were of good credit. In June, 1829, Biddle justified a loan to Congressman Verplanck, against the objections of Robert Lenox, partly on the ground that it was expedient for the institution to stand well with those who held its future existence in their hands, especially as he believed that "the loan was perfectly safe." In 1831 he permitted John Forsyth to borrow a large sum at a long date on the security of a mortgage, though such loans were against the declared policy of the bank. A similar accommodation was granted to George McDuffie in 1833, for $100,000, the agreement being to loan on mortgage and to renew the note in-

definitely. David Crockett's bill was about to be protested, and was renewed by Biddle personally to protect Crockett, and the same favor was accorded Joseph Vance. In 1826 the board released Senator Samuel Smith from his debt consequent upon the Baltimore frauds of 1817–19. Asbury Dickins, first clerk in the treasury and a valuable friend, was released in 1830, the bank saving about half the debt. Colonel R. M. Johnson and his brother were treated with like kindness in 1824. All these were favors to men who might be politically useful. Moreover, during the years when the bank was attempting to secure a new lease of life, the loans to congressmen were large, and much beyond what had been customary at earlier periods.

It must be remembered, however, that all the loans of the bank were much more extensive than usual at this time, and hence those of congressmen might fairly be expected to be so. Similarly, in settling the debts due when the debtor could not pay, congressmen were not the sole recipients of such favor, but shared it with hundreds of others. Therefore no censure is implied where the favor was not unduly granted, and the evidence of the president's letter books is conclusive that in all the cases named full payment could not be made. Smith's debts had been contracted in 1817–19 through the criminality of his mercantile partner, and he could not discharge them; Johnson's indebtedness had been incurred at the same time and he was entirely bankrupt; while Dickins's debt had been contracted with the Bank of Columbia, and he was never in a situation to pay it.

On the other hand, in the matter of granting unusual loans to congressmen, the bank seems to have laid itself fairly open to censure. Yet much of this must be mitigated if the loans were safe.

Tyler's committee in 1834 reported on this head that of loans made by the Philadelphia office to individuals then in Congress only $400 had been carried to the account of "suspended debt" and one note for $500 protested. These it considered debts which would ultimately be paid. Some cases existed at the branches, but all these loans seem to have been made "upon as good security" as was customary in other cases.

Other charges of indirect bribery were those of paying excessive fees to lawyers and making donations of the bank's money for political effect. Nothing of the kind was discovered. The fees to lawyers were not excessive. No cases of bribes by donations were known by the committee of 1834, and the subject was carefully investigated by the committee of 1832 with results favorable to the bank, the whole amount of donations from 1817 to 1831 aggregating $4,620. The contributions were insignificant and were made for the most part to fire companies, or to turnpikes, with the object of increasing the value of real estate held by the bank or of protecting its property.

The most effective of all the indictments against the bank was that it "subsidized the press." This was a vague phrase, but it was pretty clearly understood by everybody and meant that the bank bribed printers and publishers by granting them accommodations on easy terms, with the expectation of receiving their assistance in return. Of course, editors occasionally needed bank accommodations, yet, as professed molders of public opinion, they were first to take sides either for or against the bank when the subject of re-charter came up. In this situation, a loan to an editor favorable to re-charter would be called a subsidy, a loan to an editor opposed a bribe. The most prominent editors to secure large loans were Duff Green, of the Washington *Telegraph,* Webb and Noah, of the New York *Courier and Enquirer,* Gales and Seaton, of the *Intelligencer,* Robert Walsh, of the *National Gazette* and the *American Quarterly Review,* Thomas Ritchie, of the Richmond *Enquirer,* Jesper Harding, of the Pennsylvania *Enquirer,* and F. B. Blair, of the *Globe,* though before he established that paper. All were prominent and able editors, some favorable to the bank, some opposed. Suspicion was also aroused by the conversion to the bank's cause of several editors who had been unfriendly. Duff Green ceased to oppose; while Webb and Noah became active supporters instead of bitter opponents.

Numerous cases of attempts to buy up editors were also alleged. Parton intimated that such an attempt was made on Blair. Blair himself makes charges of this character in reference to the New York *Evening Post* and the New York *Standard,* and presents the affidavit of a country editor declaring that "a supporter of the Whig, or Bank candidate" offered him $100 and banking facilities at the Bank of the United States if he would use his influence for the Whig candidate. It is apparent that all this evidence is of the flimsiest, and does not establish in a single instance any connection of the bank with the alleged attempts. In one case "a known friend of the bank" offers a loan, in another "Silas E. Burrows" promises "valuable pecuniary consideration," and in the third it is "a supporter of the Whig" candidate. That there were editors who were not averse to receiving favors scarcely needs to be said. James Gordon Bennett, who always displayed in public the most rancorous antipathy for the bank, nevertheless kept up a friendly correspondence with its president, gave good advice, and on one occasion defined his position thus: "Of course I am opposed to the Bank and must be so — but I suppose you understand that." Three weeks later he hints that he needs money and would like to hear from Biddle. The bank had nothing for him, however.

Biddle's own attitude in relation to "subsidizing" the press has been incidentally left on record by himself, and does honor to his integrity. In 1828 Webster urged upon him the expediency of granting loans to Gales and Seaton in order to sustain their newspaper, which might be useful to the bank. To this Biddle responded warmly that he could not and would not proceed on any such principles:

The value of his paper and the advantage of its continuance are considerations entirely foreign to us — and the very circumstance that but for the Bank of the United States any newspaper would be discontinued, or that the Bank had gone out of its way in order to sustain any newsaper either in administration or in opposition would be a subject of reproach and what alone makes reproach uncomfortable of just reproach.

As this letter was never intended for the public eye, it is the best possible testimony to Biddle's integrity at the time it was written. And yet it was the untoward fate of the man who wrote it, and who in so doing denied accommodations to old and trusted friends at a critical moment in their fortunes and risked offending an intimate and powerful advocate, to be generally regarded as a wholesale briber of editors and publishers.

Of all the loans to editors, those to Webb and Noah, of the New York *Courier and Enquirer*, gained the widest notoriety and created the most intense feeling. This journal had been pro-

nouncedly anti-bank from November, 1829, to April, 1831. It then changed its attitude and advocated a new charter with modifications, though still professing to support Jackson.

James Gordon Bennett, in his *Memoirs*, declares that the paper was financially embarrassed in 1831, and that Noah, seeing "the breeches pocket of Mr. Biddle open, entered it immediately." It is not necessary to credit Bennett with extraordinary veracity, but he was probably not far wrong. Certain it is that in the spring of 1831 the proprietors of the paper needed more funds, and one of them decided to sell out. At this juncture M. M. Noah, who was desirous of buying up the retiring proprietor's shares, met with Silas E. Burrows, and Burrows, Webb, and Noah planned to raise the necessary means, and "to change the tone of the *Courier and Enquirer*" — in other words, to bring it out in support of the bank. Burrows was the pivot upon which all the succeeding events turned. He was a vain, loquacious, intruding, scheming merchant, who wished to be regarded as one who bore upon his shoulders the burden of empires. His letters to Biddle are still extant, and are filled with hints of mysterious secrets; chatter of grandiose plans; fulsome laudation at one moment and causeless reproaches at the next; abject petitions for loans to be used in airy ventures; denunciations of the officials of the New York branch; tales of intimacies with presidents and ex-presidents; boasts of imaginary influence over the course of politics; and again with exclamations of fear and violent assertions that he is a persecuted and hunted man. They portray only too clearly an individual possessed of an incurably weak head.

When the trio began operations for securing complete possession of the *Courier and Enquirer*, Webb mentioned to Burrows that he "was prepared to advocate a modified recharter of the bank." Burrows urged him to come out for an "unconditional recharter," and promised Noah that he would raise the funds for the purchase of the half interest in the *Courier and Enquirer* by securing a loan from his father. This proposition was accepted, and Burrows hurried off to Philadelphia to see Biddle, with the object of securing the money there instead of from his father. He told Biddle that he wanted $15,000 for Noah to purchase "a share in a newspaper," and offered the notes of Noah, indorsed by Webb, as security. The Exchange Committee of the bank authorized the loan at one year and eighteen months. Biddle then furnished Burrows with the money out of his own pocket, without even seeing the notes to secure the sum, and consenting that Burrows should not indorse them thus leaving the responsibility of payment with Noah and Webb. The truth is that Burrows did not then have the notes, for he took the $15,000 to New York, told Noah that he had secured a loan from his father, gave Noah his father's notes instead of the money, took Noah's notes, and then sent them to Biddle, who held them in his own possession for over nine months instead of placing them in the possession of the bank. Here, then, was a large loan made without the receipt of any security at the time on the notes of one partner indorsed by the other — an act in contravention of the rules of the bank; not indorsed by the borrower; and for a long period.

In January, 1832, Biddle at last decided to transfer the account to the books, and then the notes, instead of being for one year and for eighteen months, were transformed into paper to be paid at intervals of six months until October,

1836; that is, for from six months to almost five years. In February the investigation of the bank was discussed in Congress, and on the 2d of March Burrows took up the notes, securing a loan at the bank for the purpose, so that the loan made to Webb and Noah was paid by making a new one to Burrows.

The precise relations existing between Biddle and Burrows cannot be determined. In the spring of 1831 Burrows had persuaded Biddle that he was a person of vast though undefined influence in New York politics, and as at that moment the legislature of New York was discussing a resolution denunciatory of the bank, Burrows went to Albany to attempt to prevent the action. It was then that the agreement was made with Webb and Noah. As Burrows could not keep silent, the matter was at once bruited in the public press, whereupon Biddle wrote, asking Burrows to send him a letter saying that he had never "received any authority . . . from any one connected with the Bank to influence by pecuniary or other means the course of any newspaper in New York or elsewhere." Burrows did not furnish this certificate of good character; but, on the contrary, denominated himself "your agent, confidential agent," and later, in a letter of passionate, childish, and desperate reproach, angrily asserted that he was refused accommodations "whilst the Bank has stifled the press here by rewards of fortunes," and transmitted a bill for services which shows that Biddle had paid him $16,000 and still owed him $1,100. One week later he forwarded another long letter of reproaches, and hinted that he held secrets which would bring a fortune to himself and ruin to the bank; in March, 1832, on the other hand, he wrote Biddle: "All discounts made at your bank to me, have been for my accommodation, and individual benefit. Beyond this is unknown to you, and is left for me to explain." He would not appear before the congressional investigating committee, however, and "hopes to God" he will not be called on, and then exclaims: "The moment I knew you had made an entry of these documents, that moment I knew a fortune was at my disposal if I would accept of it, and made without censure by the world, as they would justify me for testifying to all."

It is difficult to assert anything with confidence in the face of such declarations from a man of this character. Burrows may really have thought that Biddle had agreed with him to bribe the New York press; the sums which Biddle had intrusted to his keeping show that he was actually acting for the bank in some capacity; his remarks about the money loaned to him prove that Biddle did not know what he had done with it, and the testimony of Noah and Webb shows that he did not transfer it to them. Biddle's friends evidently regarded Burrows as a bad character, for Bevan writes of him as "a troublesome and unprincipled man," and later as "a very dangerous man, and one in whom no confidence can be placed," at the same time expressing a wish that arrangements "could be speedily made to get W. and N.'s paper out of his possession."

Webb and Noah were accommodated with other loans. In August, 1831, they received $20,000, payable 10 per cent. every six months. They declared that they could not secure loans from the New York banks because they had supported the bank. On this occasion Noah said that their paper would, if it took part in the agitation for re-charter, "go as far in favor of the bank" as it had done in April. In December the partners were

back once more, this time for $15,000, claiming that the bank was morally bound to support them, because their course had cut them off from assistance from the New York banks. The loan was granted by the Exchange Committee, though at the time the board was refusing to lend small sums to good customers in Philadelphia. In both cases the notes were drawn by one partner and indorsed by the other.

Nor was this the end. In July, 1832, after the veto, Biddle twice brusquely refused further accommodations to Webb, whereupon that gentleman threatened that unless something was done for him the paper would support Jackson. Biddle then consented to see if the loan could not be raised by one of his friends, for which kindness he received the thanks of Webb. Whether anything was done or not is unknown, but Noah retired from the *Courier and Enquirer*. Webb removed the names of Jackson and Van Buren from the head of the editorial columns of the paper and came out in a long article for Clay, Sergeant, and the bank. Let it be added that Webb's notes for $18,600 went to protest in February, 1833, and that in 1835 he offered to settle for ten cents on the dollar. It does appear as if Biddle had become sadly involved with the *Courier and Enquirer* and could not extricate himself. The loans granted to the editors of this paper would assuredly not have been made to others unless similarly situated.

It is easy to conjecture the arguments which appealed to Biddle in this matter. He had openly announced his belief in the policy of disseminating knowledge of the bank through the press, and of the justice of paying for such publications. In this policy he was supported by men of the most irreproachable character, and it may be added that after the beginning of the campaign of shameless slander and calumny inaugurated by Blair, he was certainly not without justi- fication, and would have been more than an ordinary mortal had he done otherwise than he did. But it was only one step from this legitimate policy to that of making loans as a sort of payment for publications, and perhaps this subtle logic appealed to Biddle. He might re- gard such loans, even if it could be pointed out that they were not justified by business considerations, as justified by the resolution of the bank to pay for publications. If he had been willing to pay the *Courier and Enquirer* several hundred dollars for the publication of a few columns in a single issue, what pos- sible objection could there be to a loan of $52,000 which would secure every issue of the paper for the bank's cause? As a matter of economy the second method might even be preferable to the first, since there was a chance of securing the repayment of the capital with in- terest, besides having the support of the paper.

Payments made to printers by the bank for publishing documents, articles, and speeches favorable to re-charter were open to the criticism of being politi- cal; outside the province of a bank; made out of the money of the stockhold- ers, the largest of whom was the govern- ment of the United States itself; and, finally, virtual bribes to the fortunate printers and editors who received the jobs. While the directors felt justified in making these expenditures, yet all these objections were valid, even supposing that the prices paid for the work done were not excessive. Everyone knows that the securing of printing which yields a fair profit is a matter of much moment with publishers, and that those who fur- nish such business are naturally treated

as patrons. In reference to compensation, the Senate committee of 1834 declared that the bank had given no gratuities to printers or publishers, and left it to the Senate to judge whether or not the insti- tution had allowed them "extra compen- sation." The evidence proves that the rate of payment was moderate.

Another objection to the expenditure was that the president of the bank was permitted to dispose of the funds at his own discretion. Jackson bitterly com- plained of this in his paper of September 18, 1833, declaring on the authority of the government directors that the sums spent by the bank for printing "during the years 1831 and 1832 were about $80,000." The directors, said Jackson, put "the funds of the bank at the dis- position of the president for the purpose of employing the whole press of the country in the service of the bank, to hire writers and newspapers, and to pay out such sums as he pleases to what person and for what services he pleases without the responsibility of rendering any spe- cific account." The criticism was just. The expenditures for extra printing from 1829 to 1834, inclusive, aggregated $65,103.25, and to these were added ex- penditures by President Biddle, without vouchers, and without designation of the purposes for which they were made. The total of these was $29,605. In whatever light the first of these items may be viewed, the second was totally indefen- sible. The Senate committee of 1834, though favorable to the bank, con- demned the practice and virtually cen- sured the directors for allowing the presi- dent to exercise such powers under the resolution of March 11, 1831.

It is to Biddle's credit that he never made any mystery of his policy in regard to paying for publications in the news- papers, and willingly gave his reasons for it. He believed that most of the opposition to the bank was due to ignorance, and that explanatory articles would dispel this ignorance and so put an end to the opposition. Thoroughly convinced that this was true, he continued publishing. He was assuredly mistaken. Ingersoll in 1831 gave it as his opinion that not three members of the Pennsylvania legislature had ever "read or will ever read McDuffie's report, Gallatin's article or the views in the North American and the National Gazette"; while in 1834 Mathew Carey declared that the system of issuing pamphlets dealing with abstruse banking questions at great length was utterly mistaken, that nobody would read them, or, if anybody did, that he would not understand them. This judgment seems sound, as anyone will agree who has read the pamphlets.

The amount of published matter paid for by the bank was very great. It began in April, 1830, with Senator Smith's report, and continued for about five years. The bank not only published articles itself, but distributed those of others, and paid newspapers to publish reports. As a consequence, everyone who wrote on banking subjects wanted the bank to pay for his publication. In one case, at least, a pamphlet was published without the privity of the bank, and then recompense was demanded. Newspapers, of course, would not print articles supporting the bank without compensation. A congressman rarely made a friendly speech without expecting its dissemination at the expense of the bank. The most amusing case is that of John Tyler. Tyler was chairman of the Senate investigating committee of 1834, and, voicing the austere public morality characteristic of Virginia Republicanism since the days of Jefferson, criticised the bank for disseminating pamphlets and congressional re-

ports. "Our friend," wrote Webster, "seemed to reserve all his censure for these heads." Biddle, therefore, felt quite safe in asking Tyler if he wished his report disseminated. The surprise and disgust of the bank's president may easily be guessed when he discovered that Tyler did wish it to the extent of a thousand copies. Whatever credit is due Tyler for his political morality, a sense of humor was evidently not [one of] his prominent characteristics.

That the matter of printing was carried entirely too far will easily be gathered from what has been said, and even the bank's most eager partisans were convinced that this was so. Watmough, who arranged for much of the printing, at last protested. He thought they should cut down the number of congressional speeches published, though he added, with bitter pleasantry, "It is a great assistance to Green, to be sure. He is at best however but a *mauvais sujet,* and scarcely worth what has already been done for him." The printers, in his opinion, were "pretty much all alike — let them handle the money, *au diable,* the rest."

The charge of jobbing in public stocks touched the honor of the president and corporation, and, if proved, established a violation of the law; for the charter declared that the corporation should not "purchase any public debt whatsoever," or sell "more than $2,000,000 thereof in any one year." The specific charge was that the bank jobbed in the 3 per cent. stock, and that in doing so it had interposed to prevent the payment of the national debt by urging the government's creditors not to present the certificates of the stock when the day of payment came.

The facts were as follows: On the 24th of March, 1832, Asbury Dickins, acting secretary of the treasury, informed

Biddle that one-half of the 3 per cents., amounting to $6,500,000, would be paid off by the government on the 1st of July. The bank would have to furnish the funds from the government deposits held. Unfortunately, the discharge of the debt in this year had been so enormous, and the bank's business so expanded, that it was impossible to raise the sum required by the date specified. Biddle, long before the notice from Dickins, had attempted to reduce the bank's business and so get possession of sufficient specie to meet the government's demands. He had failed in this attempt. He accordingly looked about him for some other means of evading the threatened embarrassment, which would be fatal if it occurred in the midst of the campaign for a renewed charter. Hurrying to Washington, he requested as a temporary relief a postponement of the payment from July 1 to October 1, and offered, on behalf of the bank, to pay the interest on the stock for the three months. His request was granted on this condition. Later the treasury concluded to discharge two-thirds of each certificate in October, and the remainder of the debt on January 1, 1833, thus calling upon the bank for a sum of $13,000,000 within three months' time.

The bank's difficulties under these circumstances are vividly portrayed in the correspondence with the branches, and in a letter of Biddle's to Cadwalader, outlining his plan to secure the means of payment. Biddle thought that local discounts must be diminished wherever possible; that dealings in internal exchange should be materially reduced; that as much money as could be spared should be used to discount paper secured by a deposit of 3 per cent. stock and to purchase bills of foreign exchange; and that negotiations should be begun with

holders of the 3 per cents. Cadwalader was doubtful as to the adequacy of this plan, and it was evident that the principal reliance must be in a negotiation with the holders of the stock, in which the bank would secure a loan by paying the interest on the stock in the place of the government, the holders accepting its responsibility and thus relieving the government from all liability. Any other form of loan at this time was hardly feasible, since no one wished to lend.

The board of directors had already authorized the president and the exchange committee to defer "a part of the payments." Proceeding in accordance with this authority, the following plan was adopted: The certificates of foreign holders of the stock were to be surrendered to the bank and by it passed over to the government as evidence of the payment of the debt. The bank itself, however, would not pay the principal, but borrow it from the original holders of the debt, continuing the loan for another year in place of the government and paying the interest during the continuance. The payment of $5,000,000 of the stock was thus to be deferred. To this plan there could not be the least possible objection, either legal or moral, since the government would be discharged of all obligation, the bank simply procuring a new loan to the extent of the $5,000,000 on its own responsibility. The operation would be the same as if it had paid the debt outright and then immediately borrowed it back from the original holders on its own account.

On the day that the directors authorized the postponement of the stock, Biddle opened negotiations with T. W. Ludlow, of New York, but soon perceived that there was little chance of getting the transaction settled in time to be of service. He therefore dispatched

General Cadwalader to England to make arrangements with the Barings to defer the payment of $5,000,000 of the stock. This mission succeeded. The Barings agreed to invite the foreign holders of the 3 per cents. to retain their stock until October, 1833, while the Bank of the United States was to continue the payment of the interest quarterly and to pay the principal at the date named. Since this would probably not suffice to defer $5,000,000, as much of the stock as possible was to be bought up by the Barings for the bank, at the best terms, not over $91 on $100. The certificates were to remain with the Barings, or with the holders of them.

It will be noticed that this arrangement differed considerably from the first plan of the bank, inasmuch as the Barings were authorized to buy stock for the bank, and also to withhold the certificates, which would leave the debt still unpaid. The bank would be culpable in both particulars, for it was prohibited by its charter from purchasing any public debt, and the arrangement for deferring the delivery of the certificates was an unjustifiable interference with the government's plan to discharge the debt. Cadwalader's agreement was, therefore, both morally wrong and illegal. But this would not necessarily involve the bank, for the vital question was: Had he authority to make such an agreement? In answer to this question Cadwalader distinctly averred that he alone was responsible, his instructions not having contemplated the purchase of the stock. In support of his admission are the declarations of the directors that no such agreement was contemplated, and Biddle's disavowal of that part of it which was patently illegal on the ground that the institution was forbidden by its charter "to purchase any public debt

whatsoever." Unless there was an infinite amount of shabby lying, and that, too, under oath, the corporation was not guilty. The presumption that everybody lied will hardly be considered tenable.

The disavowal of Cadwalader's contract gave rise to new complications. Biddle insisted that the certificates of the stock must be sent to the United States in order that he might turn them over to the secretary of the treasury. The Barings had already purchased $1,428,974.54 and got $2,376,481.45 postponed. They now concluded to buy the latter also if the owners would not consent to the bank's revised terms, which were to the effect that new certificates should be given for the old ones surrendered, the bank to continue paying the interest. Many of the foreign holders agreed to these terms, and the Barings secured their certificates and forwarded them to the United States.

The affair made a great noise, and kept the bank's advocates busy explaining for many months. Biddle was particularly sensitive about the charge of violating the charter. That the bank should encourage the holders of the debt not to present the certificates for payment, he apparently considered of little importance and of no concern to anyone but the bank. Writing on the subject he revealed the depth and the keenness of his feeling:

With regard to the return of the certificates the Government cannot oblige any body to present his certificate—the Government stops the interest—but cannot compel a stockholder to take his principal. . . . But supposing that the certificates are delayed for a few months, what harm does that do to any body? The interest has stopped—the money remains in the Treasury; so that instead of depriving the Government of the use of its funds, directly the reverse is true, for the Government retains the funds and pays no interest.

But that the bank, the agent of the government, should urge the holders to delay presentation of the certificates, when its business was to procure them for the government at once, was another proposition, and one not to be justified by such arguments. Moreover, the assertions that "the money remains in the Treasury," "the Government retains the funds," were not strictly true, unless the bank and the treasury were identical, for the bank retained the funds and the government had no further use of them.

Suspicious souls will consequently continue to believe that Biddle's explanations were not veracious, but in morals as in law it is well to give the accused the benefit of the doubt. The evidence of the bank's integrity was sufficient for J. Q. Adams, Gulian C. Verplanck, Albert Gallatin, and Thomas Cooper, and may well be accepted. What is certain is that after Biddle's disavowal the bank returned to its legal position, if it had ever deliberately left it, and the postponement of the 3 per cents. did not take place.

The most serious charges from the point of view of proper and safe business were those which imputed usurpation of the authority and power of the board of directors, by the president and the exchange committee, and the use of such power to loan funds to favored individuals on unusual terms.

The charge of loaning large sums of money to favorites was made in the case of T. Biddle & Co. The bank replied by asserting that the firm acted as its brokers, which is undoubted, and that the loans were made to them to loan for the bank. This is likely. Professor Sumner's assertion that precisely such loans led later to the ruin of the bank is not apropos, because the later loans were made deliberately at a moment when it was intended to close up the bank's business, and were of an entirely different nature.

The president of a bank, if he is a real and active executive, a man of energy, of autocratic temper, of tact and skill, will always secure power over his board, provided that he wishes to do so. In the case of the Bank of the United States this was rendered easier by the position of the president. Under the by-laws he was *ex officio* a member of every committee. This power in committee was increased by his right under the rules of 1833 to name them all with one exception. In addition it must be recollected that his tenure of office was continuous, while that of the directors was intermittent. Again, most of the voting for directors was done by proxy, and out of 4,533 proxies in 1832, Biddle in person held 1,436, and was joint holder in the case of 1,684 others. While he thus held a controlling number of the votes of distant stockholders, those resident in Philadelphia rarely attended elections, and consequently the holders of proxies had power to elect the directors if they chose.

Nicholas Biddle was a man of intense energy, autocratic in temper, and possessing supreme confidence in his own judgment. It was inevitable that he should rule and not merely reign, and the proofs that he did rule are observable everywhere. He appointed the committees of the bank after 1828, though the rules giving him this power were not adopted until 1833; he does not want the bank's books examined by the government directors, and he gives orders that the books must not be examined by them, though only the board could rightfully do this; he desires new directors at the central board and writes, "General Cadwalader and myself have thought it was for the interest of the Bank to make the change," though it would be difficult to find in the charter any clause giving General Cadwalader and Nicholas Biddle authority to appoint new directors.

Though such power might not in itself be objectionable, it was certainly liable to abuse, and under Biddle something like abuse can be detected. The most serious charge was that of R. M. Whitney, who asserted in 1832 that the president of the bank (1) made discounts on his own authority; (2) that in doing so he favored his relatives, T. Biddle & Co.; (3) that he made such loans without charging interest; (4) that a custom had obtained of permitting brokers to receive money from the teller's drawer as temporary loans, leaving stock certificates as security; (5) that these transactions were not entered on the books of the bank, and consequently never came to the knowledge of the directors. To substantiate his charges, Whitney told a very circumstantial story to the effect that the cashier and assistant cashier had reported to him specific transactions of this character in May, 1824; that he with them went to the first teller's drawer and found security for two temporary loans of large sums; that they then went to the discount clerk's desk and found two notes for large sums which had been discounted by the president alone, and not entered on the books. He said that he instructed the officers "to enter on the books the money that had been loaned from the Teller's Drawer," and that this was done under the head of "bills receivable"; that he then went at once to President Biddle and "desired that nothing of a similar nature should occur while" he remained a director. The president "colored up a good deal" and said that there should not. Whitney had taken a memorandum of the sums at the time and produced it

in corroboration of his assertions. He gave exact dates for the transactions.

Unfortunately for him, his evidence broke down at every one of the essential points most needing corroboration. In regard to the charge that the president made discounts on his own authority, ex-Cashier Wilson, who was said to have given the information and was summoned to support Whitney, swore positively that the notes referred to had been discounted by the board and not by the president. Both the officers who, Whitney asserted, had communicated to him the facts about the loan swore that they had no recollection of such an interview. The first teller and the discount clerk declared that they had no knowledge of the alleged visit to their desks. The officers also swore that no single director had authority to order entries made on the books, and in case such an order was given no clerk would obey it. Mr. Andrews furnished evidence in the books to show that the sum of $45,000 was actually entered on the day the loan was made, and consequently could not have been ordered entered by Whitney. In regard to the charge of favoritism to the Biddles, the evidence adduced was conclusive that the president had not been guilty. That interest had been paid on all accommodations granted to the firm was irrefutably established by the testimony, by the books of the bank, and by those of the firm of T. Biddle & Co. Finally, to Whitney's complete discomfiture, it was proved that President Biddle was in Washington when the particular loans referred to were made in Philadelphia, and so could not have made them, nor could he have been interviewed then by Whitney in regard to the loans. The entire case was so overwhelmingly against Whitney that he was compelled to admit that the two loans were not made by the president; that the interview with him so confidently alleged did not take place at the time stated; that interest had been paid on the loans; and that he was not sure that he had directed the entries to be made. The committee, though hostile to the bank, passed a majority resolution declaring that in their opinion the charges were "without foundation."

Yet before the very committee which heard these charges and admitted their disproof, it was proved beyond question that the president of the bank had on his own responsibility bought bills of exchange; that he had granted interest to T. Biddle & Co. on loans by them to the bank, without the consent of anyone and against the protests of the cashier; that on March 23, 1832, he had discounted a note for $3,500 for General Stevens, a congressman and a stranger to him, without consulting either the exchange committee or the board, and this in spite of the fact that the board met the same day. In May, 1831, Biddle also granted a loan to the War Department, though he had "had no opportunity of consulting the Board of Directors on the subject."

These cases are, however, the only ones which a thorough search has revealed. Nor would it be rational to expect that many cases existed, since Biddle was so autocratic that his will would be pretty certain to obtain at the board. This was particularly likely because the directors rarely attended a session of the board in any number. On one occasion McIlvaine writes Biddle that no quorum could be secured, and on another he says, "we had the unusually large Board of eight this morning." With a directorate so little devoted to the irksome duties of their positions, it was inevitable that power should fall into the hands of a few, and it is not surprising to find an acquaintance appealing to Biddle for a loan on the ground that "you always get your way with the Board."

Even if Biddle had not controlled the board, still he might easily control the committee of exchange, which was small and appointed by himself, and over which he presided. The essential charge was that this committee supplanted the board completely. That the committee itself had no reason for existing could not be urged, since the purchase and discounting of bills of exchange might frequently need to be made between discount days, and the board met only twice a week. Horace Binney consequently upheld the exchange committee as indispensable "to the due management of the parent bank." The question still remains: Did it act as the agent or the master of the board?

The exchange department was created early in the history of the bank, and a committee to manage the department naturally followed. As exchange operations were at first very limited, the committee was of little weight; but with the stupendous growth of such dealings under Biddle's system it became very important. It was now appointed quarterly by the president, though down to 1828 it had been selected by rotation, so that all members might sit upon it. In the early days, too, the functions of the committee consisted in the management of only exchange operations, while in 1832 an officer of the bank could say that "the principal object of having the Exchange Committee" was to discount notes on days that the board of directors did not sit. At this time the committee purchased "bills both foreign and domestic, and, in the absence of the Board," discounted "domestic bills on any part of the United States." It also discounted promissory notes. In brief, it might "be said, in some measure, to represent the board . . . to act for the board" even in the ordinary business of the bank. In acting, however, it was authorized by votes of the directorate, sometimes to perform specific duties, as in the case of the 3 per cents., sometimes to operate generally, as by the resolutions of the 9th of July, 1830, which authorized the committee "to loan on the collateral security of approved public stock, large sums of money, at a rate of discount not lower than five per cent." The government directors in 1833 objected to the making of discounts by the committee, moving to restrict it to exchange purchases; but, nevertheless, the board as a whole approved.

Such authority and such powers might not be objectionable, provided that the board kept itself informed of the transactions entered into by the committee and checked them when necessary. But the discounts were not generally "laid before the directors for their approval or rejection," but were "acted upon definitely by the committee," the directors not members of the exchange committee meanwhile knowing no "more of the nature of the operations than other persons." Such discounts were, however, entered upon the books and submitted to the board after being made, with the exception of loans on "bills receivable," which never came before it at all. In 1831, moreover, the loans on "bills receivable," that is, loans secured by stock, began to increase notably. This was ominous, when it is recollected that Biddle early in his administration had condemned such loans as bad banking. But in all this the committee acted under the board's authority.

A committee of five, including the president and cashier—a committee "expressly invested with an authority which, from its very nature, exempted" it "from many of the ordinary rules of discounting," which discounted promissory notes four days out of every week and con-

trolled the enormous exchange operations of the bank, was likely to absorb power, likely to abuse its authority. There can, indeed, be no doubt that this was the result. After the downfall of the bank, certain of the directors accused Biddle of having destroyed the institution, the specific charges being that a resolution of March 6, 1835, gave the complete control of the bank into the hands of the president and the exchange committee, that this committee exercised its authority to loan money on the pledge of the stock of incorporated companies, no matter what the companies were like or what their operations were, and that these loans ruined the bank. Biddle's accusers, however, omitted the extremely important qualification that such powers had been primarily granted to the committee five years earlier, and Biddle answered their charge that the committee dealt in regular discounts by proving that this had long been the custom, and had been authorized by the board, as is apparent enough from what has already been said. This, however, was only to push back the charges to a date five years earlier. The directors had no answer, because Biddle's rejoinder proved that they were equally guilty, having been members of the board at the time, and having voted for the obnoxious resolutions, besides declaring as members of examining committees that the business was sound. They had partly forestalled this answer, however, by declaring that the committee on the state of the bank never really investigated its affairs, but accepted statements made by the president, while many of the transactions were concealed under the item of "bills receivable." The conclusion is irresistible that abuses did exist, and were participated in by both accused and accusers. Biddle could not controvert the charge; the directors could not carry it to its logical conclusion because it inculpated them.

That abuses existed after 1830 must be admitted, and this is the principal point. But admitting this — admitting that the president and the exchange committee controlled the business of the bank, in regard to dealings in foreign and domestic exchange, to loans on stock, and to discounting between discount days, while the president even made discounts absolutely on his own authority — admitting all this, yet it does not follow that they were to be held respsonsible for the losses accruing. The board gave this authority in many cases, and, where it did not, it might have checked the practice, for the dealings of the exchange committee were placed sooner or later before the entire board, and the transactions might be known at any time. All the business of the bank was to be investigated by a committee appointed by the directors four times a year, and if this committee was efficient, all errors and all transactions should have been known to it, and through it to the board. If, therefore, bad business was done, the board, and not the president or the exchange committee, was responsible. The censure must lie here, and it must be heavy, for of all the charges examined this is the only one thoroughly substantiated, and the only one of great and perilous import.

. . . Up to the period of the Bank War, the connection between the bank and the government was an immense benefit to both, but particularly to the government. But having stated this conclusion, there is a corollary which is just as inevitable. With the growth of the Union, with the increase of national wealth and of population, the bank would have been progressively useful. From this point of view, it becomes obvious that Jackson and his supporters committed an offense against the nation when they destroyed the bank. The magnitude and enormity of that offense can only be faintly realized, but one is certainly justified in saying that few greater enormities are chargeable to politicians than the destruction of the Bank of the United States. It was the overthrow of a machine capable of incalculable service to this country — a service which can be rendered by no bank not similarly organized. Would it not be better for the nation if it could command that service today? Why should it be almost unanimously admitted that a bank of this type is of paramount importance to the finances and commerce of England, France, Germany, Austria, Russia, and yet denied that a similar bank would be of equal value to the United States? No answer to this question can be found in our political organization, none in the nature of American institutions, none in the history of our country, none in the nature of men as citizens of a republic, none in such a bank's political power; for the bank possessed no political power. In truth, there is no answer.

If, finally, it is necessary to acknowledge, in the words of Daniel Webster, that this form of a bank for the United States is an "obsolete idea," it ought, at least, to be so much the easier to understand and to admit the services which such an institution once performed at so great a profit to the people; it ought to be easy to give the due meed of praise, and no more than the due measure of blame. When this is done, it will have to be acknowledged that the old bank, in its services to the government, was far superior to any other banking system known in this country.

Bray Hammond: JACKSON, BIDDLE, AND THE
BANK OF THE UNITED STATES

MORE than forty years have passed since Catterall's monograph on the second Bank of the United States was published, and, though that account has never been superseded, it antedates all recent literature on central banking and therefore presents inadequately the public purposes of the bank. Furthermore, it includes nothing about the bank's Pennsylvania successor, which failed, and thus omits the denouement of Biddle's conflict with Jackson. The inevitable effect of the failure, in the rough justice of history, was to make Jackson seem right and Biddle wrong; and this impression, especially in the absence of attention to the purpose and functions of the bank, seems in recent years to have been strengthened. I think it needs correction.

1

The Bank of the United States — the B.U.S. as Biddle and others often called it — was a national institution of complex beginnings, for its establishment in 1816 derived from the extreme fiscal needs of the federal government, the disorder of an unregulated currency, and the promotional ambitions of businessmen.[1] The bank had an immense amount of private business — as all central banks then had and as many still have — yet it was even more definitely a government bank than was the Bank of England, the Bank of France, or any other similar institution at the time. The federal government owned one fifth of its capital and was its largest single stockholder, whereas the capital of other central banks was wholly private. Government ownership of central-bank stock has become common only in very recent years.[2] Five of the bank's twenty-five directors, under the terms of its charter, were appointed by the President of the United States, and no one of these five might be a director of any other bank. Two of its three successive presidents — William Jones and Nicholas Biddle — were chosen from among these government directors. The charter made the bank depository of the government and accountable to Congress and the Secretary of the Treasury.

On this depository relation hinged control over the extension of credit by banks in general, which is the essential function of a central bank. The government's receipts arose principally from taxes paid

[1] On the organization of the bank, besides R. C. H. Catterall, *Second Bank of the U. S.* (Chicago: The University of Chicago Press, 1903), see Raymond Walters, Jr., "Origin of the Second Bank of the U. S.," *The Journal of Political Economy,* LIII (1945), 115.

[2] The Bank of England and the Bank of France came under government ownership in 1945. The modern term "central bank" was not used till nearly a century after Biddle's death. Hamilton used the term "public bank," and the nineteenth-century equivalent was "bank of issue."

From the *Journal of Economic History,* 7 (May, 1947), 1–23, by permission of the New York University Press.

by importers to customs collectors;[3] these tax payments were in bank notes, the use of checks not then being the rule; the bank notes were mostly those of private banks, which were numerous and provided the bulk of the money in circulation; the B.U.S. received these notes on deposit from the customs collectors and, becoming thereby creditor of the private banks that issued them, presented them to the latter for payment. Banks that extended credit properly and maintained adequate gold and silver reserves were able to pay their obligations promptly on demand. Those that overextended themselves were not. The pressure of the central bank upon the private banks was constant, and its effect was to restrict their lending and their issue of notes. In this fashion, it curbed the tendency of the banks to lend too much and so depreciate their circulation.[4] Its regulatory powers were dependent on the private banks' falling currently into debt to it. The regulatory powers now in effect under the Federal Reserve Act depend upon the opposite relation — that is, upon the private banks' maintaining balances with the Federal Reserve Banks. The private banks were then debtors to the central bank; they are now creditors. The regulatory powers of the United States Bank

were simpler, more direct, and perhaps more effective than those of the Federal Reserve Banks, though they would not be so under present-day conditions.

It was notorious that large and influential numbers of the private banks and official state banks resented this regulation of their lending power. All but the more conservative found it intolerable to be let and hindered by the dunning of the B.U.S. and forced to reduce their debts instead of enlarging their loans. Many of them had the effrontery to insist as a matter of right that they be allowed to pay the central bank if and when they pleased.[5] The effort of various states, especially Maryland and Ohio, to levy prohibitory taxes on the United States Bank's branches reflects this desire of the private banks to escape regulation quite as much as it reflects the states' jealousy of their "invaded" sovereignty; the efforts were economic as well as political.[6]

In 1831, Gallatin commended the bank for its conduct during the twenties; it had "effectually checked excessive issues" by the state banks; "that very purpose" for which it had been established had been fulfilled. On the regulatory operation of the bank, "which requires particular attention and vigilance and must be carried on with great firmness and due forbearance, depends almost exclusively the stability of the currency. . . ." The country's "reliance for a sound currency and, therefore, for a just performance of contracts rests on that institution."[7] In 1833 he wrote to Horsley Palmer, of the Bank of England, that "the Bank of the United

[3] E. R. Taus, *Central Banking Functions of the U. S. Treasury, 1789–1941* (New York: Columbia University Press, 1943), Appendix III and IV; Davis R. Dewey, *Financial History of the U. S.* (New York: Longmans, Green and Company, 1931), p. 168; John Spencer Bassett, *The Life of Andrew Jackson* (New York: The Macmillan Company, 1931), p. 586.

[4] I use the term "private banks" in preference to the common term "state banks" because it brings out the essential differences between the central bank and the units of the banking system regulated by it. I therefore include as private those "state banks" proper owned in whole or part by state governments; for functionally these "state banks" proper differed little if any from the private banks.

[5] R. C. H. Catterall, *Second Bank*, p. 85.

[6] *McCulloch* v. *Maryland* (1819), 4 Wheaton, p. 315; *Osborn* v. *Bank of the United States* (1824), 9 Wheaton, p. 737. The arguments in these cases were constitutional, not economic.

[7] Albert Gallatin, *Writings*, ed. Henry Adams (Philadelphia: J. B. Lippincott and Company, 1879), III, 334, 336, 390; II, 426.

States must not be considered as affording a complete remedy," for the ills of overexpansion, "but as the best and most practicable which can be applied"; and its action "had been irreproachable" in maintaining a proper reserve position "as late as November 1830."[8] Though Gallatin did not say so, this was in effect praise of Nicholas Biddle's administration of the bank.

The powerful expansion of the economy in the nineteenth century made it necessary for the regulatory action of the bank to be mostly one of restraint, but there was occasion also for it to afford ease as holder of the ultimate reserves and lender of last resort. One of the first things it did was to end the general suspension that the country had been enduring for more than two years; and a crucial factor in the willingness and ability of the private banks to resume payment of their obligations was the pledge of the United States Bank that it would support them.[9] This, Vera Smith writes, was "a very early declaration of the view that it is the duty of the central bank to act as lender of last resort."[10]

The regulatory functions of the bank were not always well performed. Its first president, William Jones, was a politician who extended credit recklessly, rendered the bank impotent to keep the private banks in line, and nearly bankrupted it — all in a matter of three years. Langdon Cheves put the bank back in a sound condition by stern procedures that were unavoidably unpopular. When Nicholas Biddle succeeded Cheves in 1823, the

bank was strong in every respect but good will. Biddle repressed the desires of the stockholders for larger dividends, keeping the rate down and accumulating reserves. The art of central banking was not so clearly recognized then as it has since become, but Biddle advanced it, and with better luck he might well be memorable for having developed means of mitigating the tendency to disastrous, periodic crises characteristic of the nineteenth century in the United States.[11]

But Biddle, with all his superior talents, was not very discreet. He had an airy way of speaking that shocked his more credulous enemies and did him irreparable harm; and, when he described the functions of the bank, he contrived to give a livelier impression of its power than of its usefulness. Once when asked by a Senate committee if the B.U.S. ever oppressed the state banks, he said, "never": although nearly all of them might have been destroyed, many had been saved and still more had been relieved. This was ineffable in a man of Biddle's exceptional abilities. It put a normal situation in a sinister and uncouth light. A wanton abuse of regulatory powers is always possible, and abstention from it is not to be boasted of — any more than a decent man would boast of not choosing to be a burglar. By talking so, Biddle made his opponents feel sure he had let the cat out of the bag. For Thomas Hart Benton he had proved entirely too much — that he had a dangerous power "over the business and fortunes

---

8 *Ibid.*, II, 461. See also *Niles' Weekly Register*, XXXV (1828–29), 37.

9 R. C. H. Catterall, *Second Bank*, pp. 24–26; *American State Papers, Finance* (Washington: Gales and Seaton, 1858), IV, 768–69.

10 Vera C. Smith, *Rationale of Central Banking* (London: P. S. King and Son, 1936), p. 40.

11 Statements on Biddle's central-bank policy will be found in Reginald C. McGrane, *Correspondence of Nicholas Biddle* (Boston: Houghton Mifflin Company, 1919), pp. 34–36, 51, 56–58. Catterall discusses the subject admirably in his chapter v, with the limitation that central banking was no better understood in his day than in Biddle's — if as well. See also J. S. Bassett, *Andrew Jackson*, pp. 585–86.

of nearly all the people."[12] Jackson referred in his veto to Biddle's remark, and Roger Taney was still shuddering at the disclosure many years later. He believed then and he believed still, he wrote, that there was a scheme to close every state bank in the Union. He believed "that the matter had been thought of, and that the manner in which it could be done was well understood."[13] That people believed such things, Biddle had his own jauntiness, naïveté, and political ineptitude to thank.

2

When Jackson became president in 1829, the B.U.S. had survived what then seemed its most crucial difficulties. The Supreme Court had affirmed and reaffirmed its constitutionality and ended the attempts of unfriendly states to interfere with it. The Treasury had long recognized its efficient services as official depository. The currency was in excellent condition. Yet in his first annual message, Jackson told Congress that "both the constitutionality and the expediency of the law creating the bank were well questioned by a large portion of our fellow-citizens, and it must be admitted by all that it has failed in the great end of establishing a uniform and sound currency."

There is nothing remarkable about Jackson's doubts of the bank's constitutionality, for he did not defer his own judgment to John Marshall's nor, in general, had the Supreme Court's opinions attained their later prestige.[14] His state-ment that the bank had failed in establishing a good currency is more difficult to understand, for it was plainly untrue in the usual sense of the words. But he was evidently using the words in the special sense of locofoco hard-money doctrine, according to which the only good money was gold and silver; the Constitution authorized Congress to coin it and regulate its value; the states were forbidden to issue paper and the federal government was not empowered to do so. Jackson, wrote C. J. Ingersoll, "considers all the state banks unconstitutional and impolitic and thinks that there should be no currency but coin. . . ."[15] There were practical considerations no less important than the legal. It was evident to the anti-bank people that banking was a means by which a relatively small number of persons enjoyed the privilege of creating money to be lent, for the money obtained by borrowers at banks was in the form of the banks' own notes. The fruits of the abuse were obvious: notes were over-issued, their redemption was evaded, they lost their value, and the innocent husbandman and mechanic who were paid in them were cheated and pauperized. "It is absurd," wrote Taney, "to talk about a sound and stable paper currency."[16] There was no such thing. So, in Jackson's opinion, if the United States Bank was not establishing a metallic currency, it was not establishing a constitutional or sound and uniform one.

[12] T. H. Benton, *Thirty Years' View* (New York: D. Appleton and Company, 1897), I, 159.

[13] C. B. Swisher, *Life of Taney* (New York: The Macmillan Company, 1935), pp. 166–69.

[14] Even Gallatin in 1831 took pains to defend the bank's constitutionality without a reference to the court's decisions, of which he remarked in a footnote he had not known. Gallatin, *Writings*, III, 327. He was in Europe when *McCulloch v. Maryland* was decided, but not *Osborn v. Bank*

of the United States. It is notable that he would discuss constitutionality without learning till he was through that the Supreme Court had said something on the subject.

[15] R. C. McGrane, *Correspondence of Biddle*, 172. For Benton's ideas, see his *Thirty Years' View*, I, 436.

[16] J. S. Bassett, *Correspondence of Andrew Jackson* (Washington, D. C.: Carnegie Institution, 1931), V, 491; Benton, *Thirty Years' View*, I, 436.

His words might seem wild to the contaminated, like Gallatin and Biddle, but they were plain gospel truth to his sturdy antibank, hard-money agrarians.[17]

Hard money was a cardinal tenet of the left wing of the Democratic party. It belonged with an idealism in which America was still a land of refuge and freedom rather than a place to make money. Its aim was to clip the wings of commerce and finance by restricting the credit that paper money enabled them to obtain. There would then be no vast debt, no inflation, no demoralizing price changes; there would be no fluctuant or disappearing values, no swollen fortunes, and no grinding poverty. The precious metals would impose an automatic and uncompromising limit on the volatile tendencies of trade. "When there was a gold and silver circulation," said an agrarian in the Iowa constitutional convention of 1844, "there were no fluctuations; everything moved on smoothly and harmoniously."[18] The Jacksonians were even more devoted to the discipline of gold than the monetary conservatives of the present century.

There was also a pro-bank, "paper-money wing," which harbored the Democratic party's less spiritual virtues.[19] Its strength lay with free enterprise, that is, with the new generation of businessmen, promoters, and speculators, who found the old Hamiltonian order of the Federalists too stodgy and confining. These were "Democrats by trade," as distinguished from "Democrats in principle"; one of the latter wrote sarcastically in the *Democratic Review* in 1838, "Being a good Democrat, that is to say, a Democrat *by trade* (Heaven forfend that any son of mine should be a Democrat *in principle*) — being a good Democrat by trade, he got a snug slice of the public deposites."[20] Fifty years before, business had fostered the erection of a strong federal government and inclined toward monopoly; in the early nineteenth century it began to appreciate the advantages offered by laissez faire and to feel that it had more to gain and less to fear from the states than from the federal government. This led it to take on the coloration and vocabulary of Jacksonian democracy and to exalt the rugged individualism of the entrepreneur and speculator along with that of the pioneer.

The private banks and their friends had helped to kill the first Bank of the United States twenty years before, but the strength they could muster against the second was much greater. Herein lies the principal difference between the situation of the old bank when Jefferson became president in 1801 and the situation of the second when Jackson became president in 1829. Both men disapproved of the national bank and yet were inhibited by its being accepted in their own party and performing well its evidently important functions. There were also the differences that Jefferson was more amenable to reason than Jackson, that he had in Gallatin a better adviser than any Jackson had, and that the bank was under a more passive management

---

[17] The principal argument against the bank's constitutionality was not this, of course, but that Congress had no power to charter a bank outside the District of Columbia.

[18] Benjamin F. Shambaugh, *Fragments of the Debates of the Iowa Constitutional Conventions of 1844 and 1846* (Iowa City: State Historical Society of Iowa, 1900), pp. 69, 70, 71.

[19] Col. Benton on Banks and Currency, *Hunt's Merchants' Magazine*, XXXVIII (January 1858), 560–61.

[20] *The United States Magazine and Democratic Review* (Washington: Langtree and O'Sullivan, December 1838), III, 368. Alexander Hamilton's son, James A. Hamilton, a friend of Jackson and a speculator in New York real estate, seems to have been a Democrat by trade.

in his day than in Jackson's. But of most importance was the greater pressure the private banks were able to exert in Jackson's time than in Jefferson's. Between 1801 and 1829 their number had greatly increased, as had the volume of their business and the demand for credit. The records indicate that in 1801 there were 31 banks, in 1829 there were 329, and in 1837 there were 788 — an increase of 140 per cent during Jackson's administration alone.[21] These banks were associated to a marked extent with the Democratic party, especially in New York. Their opposition to federal regulation was therefore far greater in 1829 than in 1801, and it did more for Jackson's victory over the national bank than did the zeal of his hard-money locofocos. De Tocqueville wrote that "the slightest observation" enabled one to see the advantages of the B.U.S. to the country and mentioned as most striking the uniform value of the currency it furnished. But the private banks, he said, submitted with impatience to "this salutary control" exercised by the B.U.S. They bought over newspapers. "They roused the local passions and the blind democratic instinct of the country to aid their cause. . . ."[22] Without them, it is doubtful if the Jacksonians could have destroyed the B.U.S.

The Jacksonian effort to realize the hard-money ideals was admirable, viewed as Quixotism. For however much good one may find in these ideals, nothing could have been more unsuited than they were to the American setting. In an austere land or among a contemplative and self-denying people they might have survived but not in one so amply endowed as the United States and so much dominated by an energetic and acquisitive European stock. Nowhere on earth was the spirit of enterprise to be more fierce, the urge for exploitation more restless, or the demand for credit more importunate. The rise of these reprobated forces spurred the agrarians, and as business itself grew they came to seek nothing less than complete prohibition of banking.[23] Yet they chose to destroy first the institution which was curbing the ills they disapproved, and to that end they leagued with the perpetrators of those ills.[24] Jackson made himself, as de Tocqueville observed, the instrument of the private banks.[25] He took the government's funds out of the central bank, where they were less liable to speculative use and put them in the private banks, where they were fuel to the fire.[26] He pressed the retirement of the public debt, and he acquiesced in distribution of the federal surplus.[27] These things fomented

[21] United States Comptroller of the Currency, *Annual Report*, 1916, pp. 913–14.

[22] Alexis de Tocqueville, *Democracy in America*, ed. Phillips Bradley (New York: Albert A. Knopf and Company, 1945), I, 409.

[23] In a number of western states and territories they achieved prohibition: in Arkansas, Illinois, Iowa, Wisconsin, California, and Oregon — though in the last two the impetus was more than agrarian.

[24] T. H. Benton, *Thirty Years' View*, I, 158.

[25] Alexis de Tocqueville, *Democracy in America*, I, 409.

[26] Taney made himself ridiculous: he told the pet banks the government funds would enable them to lend more, he gave them checks on the B. U. S. to protect them from the monster, and then he helplessly asked them not to use the checks. — R. C. H. Catterall, *Second Bank*, pp. 302–5. United States Secretary of the Treasury, *Annual Reports* (1833), III, 369; 23d Congress, 1st Session, *Senate Document No. 16*, 321 ff.

[27] Retirement of the public debt was inflationary in that it spread a feeling of elate satisfaction and closed a field for conservative investment. Gallatin had thought the retirement would be a good thing but later found to his dismay that it was "a signal for an astonishing increase in the indebtedness of the community at large." — Henry Adams, *Life of Albert Gallatin* (Philadelphia: J. B. Lippincott and Company, 1879), p. 656.

the very evils he deplored and made the Jacksonian inflation one of the worst in American history. They quite outweighed the Maysville veto, which checked federal expenditures on internal improvements, and the specie circular, which crudely and belatedly paralyzed bank credit.

As a result, Jackson's presidency escaped by only two months from ending like Hoover's in 1933. Far from reaching the happy point where the private banks could be extirpated and the hands of the exploiters and speculators could be tied, Jackson succeeded only in leaving the house swept and garnished for them; and the last state of the economy was worse than the first. He professed to be the deliverer of his people from the oppressions of the mammoth — but instead he delivered the private banks from federal control and his people to speculation. No more striking example could be found of a leader fostering the very evil he was angrily wishing out of the way.[28]

But this was the inevitable result of the agrarian effort to ride two horses bound in opposite directions: one being monetary policy and the other states' rights. Monetary policy must be national, as the Constitution doubly provides. The agrarians wanted the policy to be national, but they eschewed the practicable way of making it that, and, instead of strengthening the national authority over the monetary system, they destroyed it.

Where they were unencumbered by this fatal aversion to centralized power, they accomplished considerable. In Indiana they set up an official State Bank, with branches, which from 1834 to 1853 was the only source of bank credit permitted and yet was ample for all but the most aggressive money-makers, who finally ended its monopoly. In Missouri, they established the Bank of Missouri, with branches, a state monopoly which lasted from 1837 to 1857, when it too succumbed to free enterprise. And in Iowa, another monopoly, the Bank of Iowa, with branches, was in operation from 1858 till 1865, when free banking penetrated the state under authority of the National Bank Act. These instances indicate that if the hard-money agrarians had had a conception of national government less incompatible with their social purposes, they might have tempered rather than worsened the rampant excesses of nineteenth-century expansion that so offended them.[29]

But as it was, they helped an acquisitive democracy take over the conservative system of bank credit introduced by Hamilton and by the merchants of Philadelphia and New York and limber it up to suit the popular wish to get rich quick. Wringing their hands, they let bank credit become the convenient key to wealth — the means of making capital accessible in abundance to millions of go-getting Americans who otherwise could not have exploited their natural resources with such whirlwind energy. The excesses of that energy have forced the Jacksonian hard-money heroics to be

---

[28] See a contemporary English observer, "Causes and Consequences of the Crisis in the American Trade," *Edinburgh Review*, LXV (July 1837), 227–28. The impetus given new banks by the prospect of closing the B. U. S. was observed everywhere. Benton exclaimed that he had not joined in putting it down in order "to put up a wilderness of local banks." — 24th Congress, 2d Session, January 1837, *Register of Debates*, p. 610. See also Jabez Hammond, *History of Political Parties in New York* (Cooperstown: H. and E. Phinney, 1846), II. 434, 489.

[29] See Hugh McCulloch, *Men and Measures of Half a Century* (New York: Charles Scribner's Sons, 1889); John Ray Cable, *The Bank of the State of Missouri* (New York: Columbia University Press, 1923); Howard H. Preston, *History of Banking in Iowa* (Iowa City: State Historical Society of Iowa, 1922).

slowly undone: the federal government's authority over money, the Treasury's close operating contact with the banking system, and the central-bank controls over credit have been haltingly restored. Credit itself, in the surviving American tradition, is not the virus the agrarians held it to be but the lifeblood of business and agriculture, and the Jacksonian hard-money philosophy has been completely forgotten, especially by Jackson's own political posterity.

3

Jackson had not committed himself against the bank during the early part of his first term but worried both those who wanted him to support recharter and those who wanted him to prevent it. In November 1829 he was friendly to Biddle and assured him that he had no more against the B.U.S. than against "all banks." The next month he slurred the bank in his message to Congress. In 1831 when the cabinet was changed, two important portfolios went to friends of Biddle: Livingston became Secretary of State and McLane Secretary of the Treasury. Both wanted the bank continued and hoped to influence Jackson. Biddle deferred to their hopes, but the tension was evidently too severe for him. The bank's enemies were growing more provocative, and in the summer of 1831 his brother, a director of the bank's St. Louis branch, was killed in a duel, more than usually shocking, which arose from the controversy over recharter.[30] What-ever the reasons, he let impatience get the upper hand and decided that the bank, without further temporizing,

should ask Congress that the charter be renewed.[31]

Jackson was offended by this direct action, and notwithstanding improvements in the new charter and concessions to his views, he vetoed the bill of renewal. The economic reasoning of the veto message was, in Catterall's language, "beneath contempt," and the most appealing allegations in it were "demonstrably and grossly false."[32] Biddle was deluded enough to have 30,000 copies printed and distributed in the bank's own interest. One may regard this as evidence of contempt for Jackson or of a faith in the democracy as sincere as Jackson's own; but it is also evidence of the limitations on Biddle's political sense. In the election that fall the bank was the leading issue, and hopes for recharter went to nothing with Jackson's overwhelming majority. Jackson's purpose now was to stop using the bank as government depository. How firmly accepted it was in Washington as the peculiar agency of the government is indicated by the resistance he encountered. He had to get rid of two Treasury heads successively before he found a third who would execute his wishes, the law giving only the Secretary of the Treasury the power to remove the government's deposits from the bank; and he had also to disregard a House resolution declaring that the government deposits were safe as they were.

With loss of the deposits, the bank lost the means of regulating the private banks' extension of credit. Biddle had made enough mistakes already, but he now made the fatal one of failing to resign and let the bank be liquidated; there is a limit beyond which the head of a

---

[30] *St. Louis Beacon*, September 1, 1831, September 22, 1831; *Niles' Weekly Register*, September 17, 1831, p. 37. The duel was fought with pistols at five feet, Major Biddle being nearsighted, and each man killed the other.

[31] R. C. H. Catterall, *Second Bank*, pp. 214 ff.

[32] *Ibid.*, p. 239.

central bank cannot decently go against the head of the government, even when he is right and the head of the government is wrong. Moreover, although a central bank is a very useful institution, it never possesses the kind of virtues that count in conflict against an intensely popular leader. By resigning, Biddle would have stultified Jackson and justified himself, as it turned out; for when the panic came in 1837, Jackson would have got the blame, with considerable justice. Furthermore, Biddle would have spared himself a tragic end. The bank was in a better condition than it came to be later, and conditions were much more favorable for liquidation, in spite of the recession of 1833–1834. Incidentally, this recession was produced, it was averred, by a vindictive curtailment of the bank's loans. There certainly was resentment mixed into the bank's policy, but on the other hand, the bank could not go out of existence, as its enemies desired, without curtailing its credit, and curtailment is always unpopular, scarcely less in a period of general expansion than in one of depression.

Instead of going out of existence the bank became a private corporation under Pennsylvania charter in February 1836, a fortnight before its federal charter expired.[33] A little more than a year later the panic of 1837 broke. It began May 10 and involved all the banks in the country, about 800 in number, with an aggregate circulation of $150,000,000 and

deposits of $125,000,000. It precipitated three distinct monetary programs — one of hard money by the anti-bank administration in Washington, one of easy money by Biddle in Philadelphia, and one of convertibility by the banks of Wall Street under the sage but incongruous leadership of the venerable Jeffersonian, Albert Gallatin.

The administration, with Van Buren now president, took the opportunity to urge an independent Treasury system, with complete "divorce of bank and state." Its course was that urged by Jackson, who wrote, July 9, 1837:

Now is the time to separate the Government from all banks, receive and disburse the revenue in nothing but gold and silver coin, and the circulation of our coin through all public disbursements will regulate the currency forever hereafter. Keep the Government free from all embarrassments, whilst it leaves the commercial community to trade upon its own capital, and the banks to accommodate it with such exchange and credit as best suits their own interests — both being money making concerns, devoid of patriotism, looking alone to their own interests — regardless of all others. It has been, and ever will be a curse to the Government to have any entanglement or interest with either, more than a general superintending care of all.[34]

Wall Street paid little attention to this program but set about preparations to resume specie payments as soon as possible, getting its own house in order and urging the banks elsewhere to send delegates to a convention "for the purpose," in Gallatin's words, "of agreeing on a uniform course of measures and on the

[33] The authorized capital of the bank under Pennsylvania charter was $35,000,000, as it had been under national charter. It appears, however, that the shares ($7,000,000 par) held by the government under the national charter were not reissued to new owners and that the actual paid-in capital of the Pennsylvania corporation was only $28,000,000. — John J. Knox, *History of Banking* (New York: Bradford, Rhodes, and Company, 1903), pp. 78–79.

[34] J. S. Bassett, *Correspondence of Jackson*, V, 495, 498, 500, 504 ff.; Condy Raguet, *Financial Register*, II (Philadelphia: Adam Waldie, 1838), 58.

time when the resumption should take place."[35]

Nicholas Biddle took a course opposed to that of both Wall Street and the administration. He demanded that the Treasury scheme be abandoned and the specie circular repealed. He contended that Jackson's policies were responsible for the financial distress and that the basic condition of recovery was their repudiation by Congress. Till these things were done, the banks should not resume redemption of their notes. Wall Street's program he denounced as premature and sacrificial. He advocated instead an active and flexible policy that should be remedial for the prostrate economy — that should check the credit contraction and the fall of prices. His own objects during the past eighteen months, he wrote James Gordon Bennett, October 1838, had been "to sustain the national character abroad by paying our debts and at the same time to protect the securities and the staples of the country from the ruinous depreciation to which they were inevitably sinking."[36] It was evident to him, he wrote John Quincy Adams in December, "that if resort was had to rigid curtailments, the ability to pay would be proportionally diminished; . . . the only true system was to keep the country as much at ease as consisted with its safety, so as to enable the debtors to collect their resources for the discharge of their debts."[37] Lenity for the banks would mean lenity for their debtors, foreclosures and bankruptcies would be avoided, and values protected from collapse. Suspension, he had already said, was "wholly conventional between the

banks and the community" and arose from "their mutual conviction that it is for their mutual benefit."[38]

The situation was one in which the more conservative settled back to let deflation, as it came to be called a century later, run its bitter course; and the hard-money agrarians sardonically joined them in hoping for the worst. But both the agrarians and Wall Street testified to the popularity of Biddle's ideas. Governor Ford of Illinois observed, with the sarcasm of a hard-money Democrat, that although the banks owed more than they could pay and although the people owed each other and the banks more than they could pay, "yet if the whole people could be persuaded to believe the incredible falsehood that all were able to pay, this was 'confidence.' "[39] In Wall Street it was said that suspension made law-breakers of every one. "Instead of the permanent and uniform standard of value provided by the Constitution, and by which all contracts were intended to be regulated, we have at once fifty different and fluctuating standards, agreeing only in one respect, that of impairing the sanctity of contracts."[40] The believers in Biddle were themselves eloquent in the new faith. Following the later debacle of the B.U.S., the Philadelphia *Gazette* said: "The immediate effect of the suspension will be an ease in the money market, a cessation of those cares and disquietudes with which the business men of our community have been annoyed. . . . . The great error . . . . to which all subsequent errors are in a measure to be traced was

---

[35] Albert Gallatin, *Writings*, III, 398.

[36] Presidents' Letter Book, No. 1, 542, Biddle MSS, Library of Congress.

[37] 29th Congress, 1st Session, *House Document No. 226*, p. 405.

[38] Condy Raguet, *Financial Register*, I, 342–46.

[39] Thomas Ford, *History of Illinois* (Chicago: S. C. Griggs and Company; New York: Ivison and Phinney, 1854), p. 227.

[40] Report of delegates to the Bank Convention, New York, November 1837; Condy Raguet, *Financial Register*, I, 229.

in the premature resumption in August 1838. . . . . The banks are just as good, and better and more solid, under a season of suspension as under its opposite."[41]

Meanwhile, the New York banks had succeeded in resuming payment of their obligations, May 10, 1838, the anniversary of the suspension. This was a real hard-money achievement, due largely to Gallatin and the Bank of England, in which the professedly hard-money administration had little if any part. Instead it had to violate with its eyes open the professions that Jackson had violated without knowing what he was doing. While still trying to distribute a federal "surplus" which had turned into a deficit, it had to resort to issues of Treasury notes, which its hard-money zealots believed unconstitutional. It had to go still further and tolerate what Biddle had demanded: the specie circular was repealed in May 1838, the subtreasury bill was defeated in June, and in July the Treasury had to accept — to its substantial relief — a credit of four to five million dollars on the books of the Bank of the United States in anticipated payment of amounts due the government in liquidation of its shares.[42] This last transaction made the bank a depository of the government some five years after Jackson had ordered

that its predecessor, a better institution, cease to be used as depository.

By the fall of 1838, banks everywhere were back on a specie basis, and, although this was mainly due to the efforts of Wall Street and Albert Gallatin, it was Biddle who had the prestige. He was riding on the crest. "All that it was designed to do has been done," he wrote John Quincy Adams in December 1838; and he was about to retire.[43] Two months later, February 1839, he was Van Buren's guest of honor at the White House. "This dinner went off very well," according to James A. Hamilton, "Biddle evidently feeling as the conqueror. He was facetious and in intimate converse with the President."[44] A month later Biddle retired from the bank, its affairs being, he said, in a state of great prosperity and in able hands.[45] The same day the directors were unanimous in describing him as one who had "performed so much and so faithfully" and was leaving the bank prosperous in all its relations . . . and secure in the respect and esteem of all who are connected with it in foreign or domestic intercourse."[46]

Six months later, in the fall of 1839, the bank suspended payment of its obligations. It resumed and then suspended again. In 1841, after two years of dismayed inquiry and recrimination, it was assigned to trustees for liquidation.

The stockholders were stunned, and then they turned on Biddle. In the summer of 1840 he was told that he owed the

---

[41] *Philadelphia Gazette*, October 10, 1839.

[42] These represented payment of $7,900,000 to the government for its stock in the bank. This sum included a premium of about $1,000,000, besides which the government had received dividends of over $7,000,000 during the twenty years of the bank's existence. The net gain to the government from its original investment of $7,000,000, which it paid for in bonds, is estimated by Knox at $6,000,000 and by Catterall at $8,000,000. — John J. Knox, *History of Banking*, p. 79; R. C. H. Catterall, *Second Bank*, p. 474. In the settlement for the government stock, agreed upon in 1837 (Catterall, *Second Bank*, pp. 373–75), the administration had held out for a premium in a way which indicated it had no doubt of the bank's solvency.

[43] 29th Congress, 1st Session, *House Document No. 226*, p. 408.

[44] R. C. McGrane, *Correspondence of Biddle*, p. 337; *Reminiscences of James A. Hamilton* (New York: Charles Scribner's Sons, 1869), p. 312.

[45] *Niles' Weekly Register*, LVI (April 6, 1839), p. 84.

[46] 29th Congress, 1st Session, *House Document No. 226*, p. 486.

bank an "over-advance" of about $320,-000 on an old account. This he denied. Nevertheless, "though he did not recognize the claim" and although "neither law or equity made it necessary to pay," he did so — mostly in Texas bonds which were accepted at more than market value. The stockholders next turned to litigation and thereafter seem to have kept Biddle continuously in the courts. In January 1842, he and former associates in the bank were arrested on charges of criminal conspiracy and put on $10,000 bail each. The charge was that they had conspired "to cheat and defraud the bank by obtaining therefrom large advances upon shipments of cotton to Europe," and "by the unlawful receipt and expenditure of large sums of money, the application of which is not specified upon the books."[47] The court of General Sessions was occupied two weeks with habeas corpus hearings, twenty witnesses being examined and "all the books and papers of the bank brought into court, where they underwent a most searching investigation." Biddle's attorney let his case stand on the evidence of the prosecutors. "As soon as the testimony for the prosecution was finished, the counsel for Mr. Biddle offered to leave the matter to the court without argument."[48] The court found evidence lacking that the acts charged involved fraud; for they were known to the directors and approved by them. Of any fraudulent coalition it found nothing to justify even a reasonable suspicion.[49] Two judges concurred in this decision; one dissented.

A few weeks later another suit was instituted. The stockholders filed a bill of equity in which they asked that Biddle and one of his former associates be required to account for $400,000 of the bank's funds. The bill was dismissed December 1844, the court holding that information which might incriminate the defendants could not be required of them.[50] But Biddle was no longer living. He had died ten months before, February 27, 1844, aged fifty-eight.

4

The failure of the B.U.S. leaves two questions one would like to have answered: What was the actual condition of the bank? How responsible was Biddle for it? The Jacksonians had easy answers, of course, and jeered triumphantly; matters had proved to be even worse than they had said, Biddle had known the bank was rotten, and having enriched himself he had striven to leap clear in time but had been caught. The Democratic press was hot with invective and ribald ridicule of the great Regulator, the old Nick, the prestidigitatorial wizard who had crowned a career of astounding performances by consummately destroying everything he had done, and himself with it.[51]

To say with Biddle's political enemies that the bank was "rotten" is putting it both vigorously and vaguely. No one can be precise in such a matter, for in a long and complicated liquidation involving suits and technical decisions respecting the admissibility of claims, the completeness of the settlement must be subject to interpretation. But, according to a trus-

47 29th Congress, 1st Session, *House Document No. 226*, 419 ff., 475 ff.; also opinion of Judge Barton, *Philadelphia Inquirer*, May 10, 1842.

48 *Philadelphia Public Ledger*, April 11, 1842.

49 *Philadelphia Public Ledger*, April 30, 1842. The court had much to say of "the singularly loose method" by which the directors had conducted the business of the corporation.

50 *Bank of the United States* v. *Biddle*, Parsons' Select Cases in Equity (Philadelphia, 1888), II, 33 ff.

51 *Democratic Review*, III (December 1838), 372–73.

tee quoted by Knox, the creditors were paid in full, principal and interest, though the bank's capital was entirely absorbed, and the stockholders got nothing.[52] This would mean a shrinkage of about one fourth of the value of the bank's assets, roughly speaking. The 7,000 bank failures in the United States in the ten years, 1921–1930, entailed estimated losses of about one third of the total deposit liabilities.[53] The comparison is crude, but I think it warrants the opinion that the condition of the B.U.S. was rotten only in a hyperbolical sense. Moreover, it is to be borne in mind that values usually diminish in liquidation, that the portfolio to be liquidated was the country's largest, and that the process, which ran to 1856, had to be undertaken in a period when buyers were not eager nor prices buoyant. The stockholders in 1841 insisted to the legislature that the bank could pay its creditors and requested lenity so that losses might be minimized.[54] These things make me think that the bank in 1839 may have been in a situation little if any worse than that which Jones had got its predecessor into twenty years before and from which Cheves rescued it.

As for the second question — Biddle's responsibility — it seems to me clear that policies put into effect by him led to the bank's failure but that he had no realization or suspicion of what was developing. The policies included prodigal loans on stocks, especially to officers and directors of the bank, heavy investments in corporate stocks and speculative bonds, and purchases of cotton and other agricultural commodities for export. The cotton transactions were undertaken in the

emergency of 1837 as a means of sustaining domestic commodity prices and providing European exchange. They succeeded initially, but once begun they were hard to stop, and they produced loss, litigation, and recrimination that was probably more damaging to Biddle himself than to the bank. The loan and investment policy was begun as early as 1835 when it looked as if the bank would have to liquidate: the active assets were converted into loans on stocks in preparation for a long period of liquidation. But when the Pennsylvania charter was obtained, the policy was not abandoned. Instead it was adapted to the vaster prospects of manifest destiny and empire building. Loans were made with a lax grandiosity. "It seems to have been sufficient," according to a stockholders' committee report later, "to obtain money on loan, to pledge the stock of 'an incorporated company,' however remote its operations or uncertain its prospects." Partly from choice and partly from the extortionate requirements of its charter — which Biddle should never have accepted — the bank also became the owner of such stocks outright; in 1840 it had shares in more than twenty other banks, some of which it wholly controlled, and great holdings in railways, toll bridges, turnpikes, and canals, besides speculative bonds issued to finance "public improvements."[55] These investments immobilized

52 John J. Knox, *History of Banking*, p. 79.

53 Federal Deposit Insurance Corporation, *Annual Report* (Washington, 1940), p. 66.

54 29th Congress, 1st Session, *House Document No. 226*, p. 533.

55 Laws of Pennsylvania 1835–36, p. 43; 29th Congress, 1st Session, *House Document No. 226*, p. 532. See report of the stockholders' committee, April 3, 1841, 29th Congress, 1st Session, *House Document No. 226*, esp. pp. 414–16, 425 ff. This report confirms, it seems to me, the opinion of Judge Barton a year later. I do not go into the cotton transactions, which Judge Barton discusses at length, because to discuss them adequately takes too much space. They show Biddle's audacity, ingenuity, and casuistry, but it is not clear that they cost the bank much, except indirectly by deterioration of management. The loan policy, though less irregular, did the bank more direct damage.

the bank's funds so that it was without active means to repay the government for its stock, to honor its $20,000,000 of circulating notes, which soon began to be rapidly presented for redemption, and to meet its charter obligations, which in five years made it divert more than a third of its capital "to purposes of the state." To meet these requirements, the bank was driven into the market as borrower, both at home and abroad. These borrowings were begun by Biddle, and his successors turned to them more and more. Hence the bank came to be progressively incurring new obligations harder to meet than the old. The pressure mounted swiftly, so that a situation of apparent comfort in the spring of 1839 had passed into one of agony in the fall. These were the six months between Biddle's retirement and the bank's suspension. The bank had for years been growing more and more illiquid, but the condition had remained concealed by confidence. Once the illiquidity was suspected, however, the bank's creditors woke up with a start, and its obligations became instantly menacing. The suddenness of the change depended not on existence of the condition but on recognition of it.

According to one view, Biddle cannot be blamed for the bank's failure — it happened six months after he had retired. Well, granted that Biddle was gone, the bank was in the hands of successors who besides being heirs to his policies had been trained in his school. And this school, according to the evidence of stockholders' reports and court records, was one of extreme administrative inefficiency. The directors, dazzled by Biddle, knew nothing and approved everything. There were special procedures for special transactions, items being carried in the teller's drawer till it was expedient to post them. Accounts of the old bank were continued on the books of

the new as if the corporate continuity was unbroken; and the notes of the old were kept in circulation by the new — a practice which particularly outraged Gallatin. It was in this atmosphere that Biddle's successors learned to manage the bank, and if they came to grief it cannot be said that it was merely because they had not his ability. He would have come to grief himself.[56]

That Biddle must bear responsibility for the bank's condition is one thing; but that he had a guilty consciousness of its condition is quite another. Although the tradition of his dishonesty is held both by the Jacksonian partisans and by some scholars, I think it rests on a trite and stiffly moralistic view of the facts. If he realized how seriously wrong things were, it was an instance of objective analysis and cold self-appraisal unique in his career. I cannot believe him capable of it. He was eminently of a sanguine disposition, as is emphasized in the characterization of him by Catterall, who has given him more attention than any other historian. Caution and modesty were probably never among his more conspicuous virtues, and Jackson's attack did not enhance them. In the years 1836 to 1839, when he was laying down a new course for the bank, he was at the height of his career, it then seemed, and flushed with victory. He had blundered when he forced the issue of recharter in 1832, and Jackson had whipped him in the elections that year, in the veto, and in the removal of the deposits in 1833. But by 1838 he seemed to have retrieved his blunder and defeat. He had found sanctuary for the bank in the Pennsylvania jurisdiction, where Jackson could only gnash his teeth

56 For some account of the bank's methods, see Sister M. Grace Madeleine, *Monetary and Banking Theories of Jacksonian Democracy* (Philadelphia: The Dolphin Press, 1943), chaps. iv and v. The author seems to believe Biddle morally culpable.

at it. He could point scornfully at the situation compounded of the panic of 1837, the specie circular, and distribution of the federal surplus. By 1839 he was the honored guest of Van Buren in the White House, and he could boast that the bank was again a government depository, that the independent Treasury scheme was rejected, and that the specie circular was repealed. He had triumphed over the Jacksonians on the points he cared most about. He even claimed credit for resumption, patronized Wall Street, and acted as the impresario of national monetary policy. It was in the fatuous mood of wishful thinking and expansive imagination stimulated by these illusive developments that he administered the bank after the failure of Jackson's attempt to annihilate him. If Biddle, at the height of his success in the winter of 1838–1839, examined his achievements objectively and concluded that all he had done mounted up to either a colossal fraud or a colossal mistake, he must have been a very remarkable character indeed. Yet that is what the tradition of his moral guilt requires one to believe. I find more credible the less dramatic possibility that, being a man of very sanguine susceptibilities, he was simply carried away by success and self-confidence, by the grand scale of his activities, and by the daily exercise of more power, as he put it, than the President of the United States possessed. I believe he had lost the faculty of recognizing his own mistakes. The series of letters he wrote in 1841 — prolix, specious, declamatory compositions in which he unconvincingly insisted that the bank had been in sound condition when he left it — seem to me the pathetic efforts of a man confounded by other things than guilt: by surprise, incredulousness, grief, anxiety,

and shock.[57] His friends were at no less a loss; the most they could say in his favor was to protest at those who had been his sycophants while hoping to prosper but who turned against him with a "malicious prosecution" when their common fortunes collapsed.[58]

The hostility of Jackson to the Bank of the United States was in the first instance a matter of principle, the bank belonging to a monetary system and to a theory of federal powers which he disapproved; but later he and his followers could allege also that the bank was rotten and Biddle dishonest. That allegation was, in fact, emphasized more than the original principle. But if the bank was not rotten and Biddle was not dishonest, then what may be called the moral grounds for Jackson's action disappear leaving no defense except in charity to his good intentions. All he did was destroy a wisely developed monetary system. The administration of that system by the B.U.S. was admirable but might have been strengthened and improved had not Jackson's views been so radical and his temper so intransigent. In particular, had his demoralizing attack never been made Biddle would not have been stimulated to undertake his later grandiose and tragic course. But the blame must be shared by Biddle. The fury and the folly of these two ruined an excellent monetary system — as good as any the country has ever possessed — and left a reckless, booming anarchy.

When the career of Nicholas Biddle is given the study its importance deserves, it may appear that the earlier part of it, when he was a central banker, was something less than brilliant and that the later

[57] 29th Congress, 1st Session, *House Document No. 226*, pp. 475–516.

[58] *Philadelphia Public Ledger*, April 1, 1842.

part, when he was an empire builder, was something worse than overweening. But, as it is, the evidence indicates an inventive, facile, dynamic person — vain and not too painfully honest under pressure — who encountered a bigoted interference with his extremely able management of an institution purposing to restrain the inflationary abuse of bank credit; who naïvely trusted the rightness of his position, contemned his adversary, defied him, and, after a smart defeat which he refused to acknowledge, achieved an illusory victory; who then, with overblown confidence in his own judgment, in the economic future of the country, and in the alchemic powers of bank credit, committed himself to empire building; who did things the ingenious if not the right way; and who reckoned on a faster and less fluctuant growth than the country actually had. In all this he went with the times. When an opposition that was locofoco on one side and laissez faire on the other overcame him, he joined the latter and likelier of the two. Having been stripped of the Hamiltonian garments of central control, he gladly put on the gayer ones of free enterprise. Yet Biddle was attracted more by the statesmanship of enterprise than by enterprise itself. As a central banker, his policy had been governed properly by public interest rather than profit.[59] As empire builder also, he led the bank into affairs of national scope and purpose.[60] He upheld the nation's foreign financial obligations. He intervened with both parties on behalf of Texas, whose government he had

financed.[61] He resisted Jackson's monetary measures with a determination more patriotic than discreet. His retirement from the bank at the age of fifty-three must have been greatly influenced, and very reasonably, by political ambitions. Only a few weeks before announcing that he would retire, he had been advised by Thomas Cooper that his candidacy for president of the United States was not immediately practicable because of the "prevailing ignorance and prejudice about banks" — the general suspension being still a recent matter — and that "some years hence" prospects might be better.[62] The bank's difficulties from 1839 on blanked out these prospects wholly. They did more. Biddle had rebounded from the earlier frustration that ended his career as central banker; from the disaster to his later career he had no power to turn. John Quincy Adams had dinner with him *en famille*, November 22, 1840, and talked long with him. "Biddle," he wrote, "broods with smiling face and stifled groans over the wreck of splendid blasted expectations and ruined hopes. A fair mind, a brilliant genius, a generous temper, an honest heart, waylaid and led astray by prosperity, suffering the penalty of scarcely voluntary error — 'tis piteous to behold."[63] He died a little more than three years later, in reduced circumstances if not insolvent.

Besides the Jacksonian view of Biddle and the view that I have opposed to it,

---

59 See his criticism of "mere men of business" as administrators of the B.U.S. — R. C. McGrane, *Correspondence of Biddle*, p. 27.

60 It will be recalled that, in his earlier literary days, he prepared a popular edition of the Lewis and Clark journals.

61 R. C. McGrane, *Correspondence of Biddle*, pp. 325, 333, 335; C. H. Van Tyne, *Letters of Daniel Webster* (New York: McClure, Phillips and Company, 1902), p. 213.

62 R. C. McGrane, *Correspondence of Biddle*, p. 333. See also earlier correspondence with Thomas Cooper regarding the presidency, pp. 272, 277–282, 293, 296, 323.

63 John Quincy Adams, *Memoirs*, ed. C. F. Adams (Philadelphia: J. B. Lippincott and Company, 1876), X, 361.

there is another I have already mentioned. Its distinction is its calm silence
about the unhappy events, whether dis-
creditable or tragic, of Biddle's last years.
In R. C. McGrane's *Panic of 1837,* the
bank's failure is alluded to, and Biddle's
connection with it is dismissed in a footnote: "It should be noted that Biddle was
now out of office, and can not be held responsible for what the bank did at this
period." In the published correspondence
of Nicholas Biddle, edited by Mr. Mc-
Grane, there is nothing that deals with
the things that made Biddle's last years
so miserably unlike those of his prime —
the bank's failure, the loss of money and
esteem, the prosecution of suits against
him. And similarly in the article on Biddle in the *Dictionary of American Biography,* no mention is made of his last
years being clouded by any trouble
whatsoever. Such reticence and piety
contrast genteelly with the bitterness he
actually suffered and with the judgment
that he belonged in jail.[64]

Two things combined to give Biddle's
fall a supererogatory blackness. One was
the sheer drama of the event. The largest
corporation in the country — one of the
largest in the world — had fallen suddenly from its splendid success into
sprawling collapse at the very feet of
the genius who had only recently with
grand gestures relinquished its management. It was a denouement that stimulated the imagination to make worse
what was already bad enough. The other
aggravation of the story came from politi-

cal motives. Biddle and the bank had
never been warmed to by the Whigs,
and Biddle's own ties were less with them
than with the Democrats, but the latter
naturally sought to make the bank seem
Whig.[65] They had great success; the
debacle helped to disintegrate the
Whigs and strengthened the Jacksonians
immeasurably. As a result, partisan
views have dominated subsequent judg-
ments and given Biddle the incidental
and thankless role of darkened background to the glories of Andrew Jackson;
and his achievements in credit policy,
especially in the earlier and more admirable phase when he was a pioneer central
banker, have been forgotten. Nowhere
has he been studied adequately in his
own right as a man of significant accom-
plishments, shortcomings, and misfor-
tunes. Yet, in intellectual capacity, force
of character, public spirit, and lasting
influence, he was comparable with any of
the contemporaries of his prime.

The withering that overtook Biddle's
fame did not extend to his philosophy
and example, which turned out to be triumphant, though with no acknowledg-
ment to him. The monetary views of
Gallatin and of Jackson are both obsolete,
but Biddle's have a sort of pragmatic
orthodoxy. He sought to make monetary
policy flexible and compensatory rather
than rigid. His easy-money doctrine had
its source in a vision of national develop-

[64] Reginald C. McGrane, *The Panic of 1837;
Some Financial Problems of the Jacksonian Era*
(Chicago: The University of Chicago Press,
1924), p. 205; R. C. McGrane, *Correspondence
of Biddle.* The Jacksonian opinion of Biddle is
reflected in Arthur M. Schlesinger, Jr.'s, *Age of
Jackson* (Boston: Little, Brown and Company,
1945), which I have not referred to in this essay
because I reviewed it in the May 1946 issue of
this Journal.

[65] It is not clear which party Biddle supposed
might make him president. The second Bank of
the United States was both nurtured and destroyed within the Democratic party. Its creators
and friends included Madison, Monroe, Gallatin,
and Crawford; its three presidents, Jones, Cheves,
and Biddle, were party members. Its greatest
enemies were likewise pillars of the party — Jackson himself, Benton, and Taney. Jackson's cabinet was divided. The Whigs championed the
bank less for its own sake than because Jackson's
course left them no choice, and they abandoned
it with relief as soon as they could. They were
not interested in having bank credit restricted.

ment to which abundant credit was essential. The majority of his countrymen have agreed with him. They have dismissed the man, but they have followed his ideas, especially his worse ones. They have shared his bullishness and his energy. They have not liked Jackson's primitive ideals of a simple, agrarian society, except in their nostalgic moods. They have not understood Gallatin's noble aversion for the fierce spirit of enterprise. They have exploited the country's resources with abandon, they have plunged into all the debt they could, they have realized a fantastic growth, and they have slighted its cost. Gallatin personified the country's intelligence and Jackson its folklore, but Biddle personified its behavior. They closed their careers in high honor — he closed his in opprobrium and bewilderment.

Arthur M. Schlesinger, Jr.: THE BANK WAR

BEGINNINGS OF THE BANK WAR

IN 1836 the charter of the Second Bank of the United States was to expire. This institution was not in the later sense a national bank. It was a banking corporation, located in Philadelphia, privately controlled, but possessing unique and profitable relations with the government. To its capital of thirty-five million dollars, the government had subscribed one fifth. It served as repository of the public funds, which it could use for its own banking purposes without payment of interest. It could issue bank notes up to the physical ability of the president and cashier to sign them; after 1827 it evaded this limitation by the invention of "branch drafts," which looked and circulated like notes but were actually bills of exchange. The Bank was not to be taxed by the states and no similar institution was to be chartered by Congress. In return for these privileges the Bank paid a bonus of one and a half million dollars, transferred public funds and made public payments without charge, and allowed the government to appoint five out of the twenty-five directors. The Secretary of the Treasury could remove the government deposits provided he laid the reasons before Congress.

1

Even advocates of the Bank conceded that this charter bestowed too much power. That staunch conservative Hezekiah Niles, writing in the heat of the fight for renewal, declared he "would not have the present bank re-chartered, with its present power . . . for the reason that the bank has more power than we would grant to any set of men, unless responsible to the people" (though he ultimately supported the Bank). Nathan Appleton, who had tried vainly to modify the charter in 1832, wrote carefully but emphatically in 1841: "A great central power, independent of the general or state governments, is an anomaly in our system. Such a power over the currency is the most tremendous which can be established. Without the assurance that it will be managed by men, free from the common imperfections of human nature, we are safer without it."[1]

There could be no question about the reality of the Bank's power. It enjoyed a virtual monopoly of the currency and practically complete control over credit and the price level. Biddle's own testimony disclosed its extent: —

Q.3. Has the bank at any time oppressed any of the State banks?

A. Never. There are very few banks which might not have been destroyed by an exertion of the powers of the bank. None have ever been injured.

[1] *Niles' Register*, May 12, 1832; Nathan Appleton, *Remarks on Currency and Banking*, 36.

To radical Democrats like Taney, Biddle's tone implied that he thought himself entitled to credit for his forbearance. "It is this power concentrated in the hands of a few individuals," Taney declared, " — exercised in secret and unseen although constantly felt — irresponsible and above the control of the people or the Government for the 20 years of its charter, that is sufficient to awaken any man in the country if the danger is brought distinctly to his view."[2]

There could be no question either about the Bank's pretensions to complete independence of popular control. Biddle brooked no opposition from within, and the government representatives sat through the directors' meetings baffled and indignant. "I never saw such a Board of *directors*," raged Henry D. Gilpin, " — it is a misuse of terms of *directed*. . . . We know absolutely nothing. There is no consultation, no exchanges of sentiments, no production of correspondence, but merely a rapid, superficial, general statement, or a reference to a Committee which will probably never report." He added, "We are perfect cyphers."[3]

Biddle not only suppressed all internal dissent but insisted flatly that the Bank was not accountable to the government or the people. In 1824 the president of the Washington branch had written Biddle, "As . . . there are other interests to be attended to [besides those of the Bank], especially that of the Government, I have deemed it proper to see and consult with the President." Biddle hotly replied, "If . . . you think that there are other interests to be attended to besides those with which you are charged by the administration of the bank, we deem it right to correct what is a total misapprehension. . . . The moment this appointment [of the five government directors] takes place the Executive has completely fulfilled its functions. The entire responsibility is thenceforward in the directors, and no officer of the Government, from the President downwards, has the least right, the least authority, the least pretence, for interference in the concerns of the bank. . . . This invocation of the Government, therefore . . . is totally inconsistent with the temper and spirit which belong to the officers of the bank, who should regard only the rights of the bank and the instructions of those who govern it, and who should be at all times prepared to execute the orders of the board, in direct opposition, if need be, to the personal interests and wishes of the President and every officer of the Government."[4]

In Biddle's eyes the Bank was thus an independent corporation, on a level with the state, and not responsible to it except as the narrowest interpretation of the charter compelled. Biddle tried to strengthen this position by flourishing a theory that the Bank was beyond political good or evil, but Alexander Hamilton had written with far more candor that "such a bank is not a mere matter of private property, but a political machine of the greatest importance to the State."[5] The Second Bank of the United States was, in fact, as Hamilton had intended such a bank should be, the keystone in the alliance between the government and the business community.

[2] *Register of Debates*, 21 Congress 1 Session, Appendix, 103; Taney to Thomas Ellicott, February 20, 1832. Taney Papers. See also Taney, Bank War Manuscript, 14–15.

[3] Gilpin to G. M. Dallas, January 26, 1833, to J. K. Kane, January 27, 1833, Gilpin Letterbooks.

[4] Biddle to Thomas Swann, March 17, 1824, *Senate Documents*, 23 Congress 2 Session, no. 17 (Tyler Report), 297–298.

[5] "Report on a National Bank," Hamilton, *Works*, III, 424.

2

Though conservative Jeffersonians, led by Madison and Gallatin, had come to accept Hamilton's Bank as necessary, John Taylor's dialectics and Randolph's invective kept anti-Bank feeling alive, and men in the old radical tradition remained profoundly convinced of the evil of paper money. Jackson's hard-money views prompted his opposition to the Tennessee relief system in 1820. "Every one that knows me," as he told Polk in 1833, "does know, that I have been always opposed to the U. States Bank, nay all Banks."[6] Benton, from talks with Macon and Randolph and his observations of the collapse of the paper system in 1819, similarly concluded that the only safeguard against future disaster lay in restricting the system; and that, to this end, the government should deal only in gold and silver, thus withdrawing support from the issues of privately owned banks.[7] Van Buren, Cambreleng, Taney and Polk more or less shared these views.

The ordinary follower of Jackson in the West also regarded the Bank with strong latent antagonism, but for very different reasons. Its policy in 1819 of recalling specie and checking the note issue of state banks had gained it few friends in any class, and, in Kentucky especially, the Relief War kept resentments alive. But this anti-Bank feeling owed little to reasoned distrust of paper money or to a Jeffersonian desire for specie. As a debtor section the West naturally preferred cheap money; and Kentucky, for example, which most vociferously opposed the United States Bank, also resorted most ardently to wildcat banking of its own. The crux of the Kentucky fight against the Bank was not the paper system, but outside control: the Bank's sin lay not in circulating paper money itself, but in restraining its circulation by Kentucky banks. Almost nowhere, apart from doctrinaires like Jackson and Benton, did Westerners object to state banks under local control.

Indeed, during the eighteen-twenties, even the Philadelphia Bank to a considerable degree overcame the Western prejudices against it.[8] In Tennessee, for example, until 1829 "both [Governor William] Carroll and the legislature favored federal as well as state banks, nor does anything in the history of the state indicate that there was any general feeling against such institutions before Jackson became President."[9] Caleb Atwater, a lusty Jackson man from Ohio and something of a professional West-

---

6 Jackson to Polk, December 23, 1833, Jackson, *Correspondence*, V, 236. Jackson told Nicholas Biddle late in 1829, "I do not dislike your Bank any more than all banks." Bassett, *Jackson*, 599. Cf. C. J. Ingersoll to Biddle, February 2, 1832: "General Jackson's antipathy is not to the Bank of the United States in particular, but to all banks whatever. He considers all the State Banks unconstitutional and impolitic and thinks that there should be no Currency but coin." R. C. H. Catterall, *Second Bank of the United States*, 185 n. All serious students of the Bank War agree that Jackson's hostility to the Bank was of long standing and based on principle, not the result of a burst of temper over the conduct of a branch at Portsmouth, New Hampshire, or elsewhere. Cf. *ibid.*, 183, 195; Bassett, *Jackson*, 589–593.

7 For Benton's account of the origin of his economic views, see his speeches in the Senate, March 14, 1838, *Congressional Globe*, 25 Congress 2 Session, Appendix, 216, and January 16, 1840, *Congressional* Globe, 26 Congress 1 Session, Appendix, 118–119.

8 This was less true in Missouri, where there was considerable hard-money sentiment which the most careful student of the question ascribes in large part to Benton's personal influence. C. H. McClure, *Opposition in Missouri to Thomas Hart Benton*, 23 n.

9 T. P. Abernethy, "Andrew Jackson and the Rise of Southwestern Democracy," *American Historical Review*, XXXIII, 70. Cf. St. George L. Sioussat, "Some Phases of Tennessee Politics in the Jackson Period," *ibid.*, XIV, 69: "though originally predisposed to hostility against the Bank of the United States, Tennessee, or rather the dominant western portion of the state, was yet quite willing to accept the benefits of a

erner, expressed a widespread feeling when he wrote in 1831, "Refuse to re-charter the bank, and Pittsburgh, Cincinnati, Louisville, St. Louis, Nashville, and New Orleans, will be crushed at one blow." Even Frank Blair's first large-scale blast against the Bank in the *Argus of Western America* after Jackson's election did not come until December 23, 1829, many months after Eastern groups had begun to agitate the question. This editorial — actually prefaced by an anti-Bank quote from a Van Buren paper in New York — appealed to the Kentucky fear of Eastern control; and all through 1830 the *Argus* continued to focus on the power and privileges of the Bank and the consequent peril to the Commonwealth Bank of Kentucky, never on the general implications of the paper system.[10]

Some writers have talked of frontier life as if it bred traits of "individualism" and equality which made Westerners mystically opposed to banks. Actually, like all other groups in the population, Westerners favored banks when they thought they could profit by them and fought them when they thought others were profiting at their expense. The Western enthusiasm for an assault on the Bank came, not from an intuitive democratic *Weltschmerz* born in the American forest, nor from a Jeffersonian dislike of banks, but from a farmer-debtor desire to throw off restraints on the local issue of paper money.

Similar objections to control from Philadelphia ranged many Easterners against the Bank. State institutions

branch of the great bank, as long as times were good and credit was easy, and only gradually listened to and joined in the attack on that institution, which was begun in the year of Jackson's inauguration."

10 Caleb Atwater, *Remarks Made on a Tour to Prairie du Chien; Thence to Washington City, in 1829*, 281; *Argus of Western America*, December 23, 1829, March 3, May 19, 1830, etc.

hoped, by falling heir to the government deposits, to enlarge their banking capital, at no expense to themselves. Special grievances multiplied the motives. The state banks of New York, for example, envied the United States Bank because its loan operations were not restricted by Van Buren's safety-fund system. New York City had long resented the choice of Philadelphia as the nation's financial capital. Thus in a fight against the Bank Jackson could expect the backing of a decent minority of the local banking interests.

But there was still another and more reliable source of support. In March, 1829, after the grim depression winter, a group of Philadelphia workingmen, under the very shadow of the Bank, called a meeting "opposed to the chartering of any more new banks." The hard times were blamed upon the "too great extension of paper credit," and the gathering concluded by appointing a committee, "without confining ourselves to the working classes," to draw up a report on the banking system. The committee, which was dominated by intellectuals, included two leading economists, William M. Gouge, editor of the *Philadelphia Gazette*, and Condy Raguet, editor of the *Free Trade Advocate*, as well as William Duane, the famous old Jeffersonian journalist, his son William J. Duane, a lawyer, Roberts Vaux, the philanthropist, Reuben M. Whitney, a disgruntled businessman and former director of the Bank, and William English and James Ronaldson, two trade-union leaders. A week later the committee pronounced its verdict on the paper system: —

That banks are useful as offices of deposit and transfer, we readily admit; but we cannot see that the benefits they confer in this way are so great as to compensate for the

evils they produce, in . . . laying the foundation of *artificial* inequality of wealth, and,
thereby, of *artificial* inequality of power. . . .
If the present system of banking and paper
money be extended and perpetuated, the
great body of the working people must give
over all hopes of ever acquiring any
property.[11]

This view was spreading rapidly
through the Middle and Northern states
of the East in the late eighteen-twenties.
The working class was no more affected
by an instinctive antipathy toward banking than the backwoodsmen beyond the
Alleghenies; but they never enjoyed the
Western opportunity of having banks
under their own control. Their opposition, instead of remaining fitful and ca-
pricious, began slowly to harden into
formal anti-banking principle. Their
bitter collective experience with paper
money brought them to the same doctrines which Jackson and Benton gained
from the Jeffersonian inheritance.

3

The war against the Bank thus enlisted
the enthusiastic support of two basically
antagonistic groups: on the one hand,
debtor interests of the West and local
banking interests of the East; on the
other, Eastern workingmen and champions of the radical Jeffersonian tradition. The essential incompatibility between cheap money and hard could be
somewhat concealed in the clamor of the
crusade. Yet that incompatibility remained, and it came to represent increasingly a difference between the
Western and Eastern wings of the party,
as the state banking group gradually
abandoned the Jackson ranks. It was,
indeed, a new form of the distinction
between Western and Eastern readings
of "equality." The West, in its quest for

11 *Free Trade Advocate,* May 9, 16, 1829.

political democracy and home rule, did
not object to paper money under local
control, while the submerged classes of
the East, seeking economic democracy,
fought the whole banking swindle, as it
seemed to them, root and branch.

The administration took care not to
offend its cheap-money adherents by
openly avowing hard-money ideas. Yet,
the drift was unmistakable, and it rendered ineffective some of Jackson's Western followers for whom the battle was
being pressed on lines they could not
understand. Richard M. Johnson, for
example, a staunch relief man and ancient foe of the Bank, served on the
House committee which investigated the
Bank in 1832; but he could take no real
part in a hearing dominated by Cambreleng's hard-money views, and, though he
signed Cambreleng's report, he confessed
later that he had not asked a question or
looked at a Bank book.[12] In general, the
Western politicians, torn between the
hard-money leanings of the White House
and the cheap-money preferences of the
folks back home, tended to pursue an
erratic course.

Only the intellectuals, who did not
have to think about re-election, effected
a quick adjustment. Amos Kendall, who
had been originally a hard-money man,
perhaps from his Eastern upbringing,
found no difficulty in reverting to his
earlier opinions. Frank Blair also rapidly shifted his ground after coming to
Washington. These were not basic re-
versals of position. Their allegiance, after
all, had been primarily to a social class,
not to a set of financial theories. The
experience of the Kentucky relief system
taught that salvation was not to be
bought so cheaply: however much inflation might temporarily benefit a frontier
state with a large debtor element, it was

12 Benton, *Thirty Years' View,* I, 241.

at best a risky expedient, imposed by political necessity; it never could serve as the basis of a national economic policy. Kendall and Blair, liberated from their local obligations, naturally turned to hard-money ideas as affording the only permanent solutions for the financial problems in favor of the non-business classes.

Thomas Hart Benton had long awaited the opportunity to fight for this solution. In the eighteen-twenties, when he fumed about the paper system, Nathaniel Macon would remark that it was useless to attempt reform unless the administration was with you. Now, at last, the administration seemed to be with him. Jackson's first message had expressed grave doubts about the constitutionality and expediency of the Bank. In 1830 the President continued to make ominous allusions to the subject of recharter. But the administration position was still not clear. Jackson's views were widely regarded as the expressions of private prejudice, not of party policy. Few people interpreted the Maysville veto as opening a campaign which might end by involving the Bank.[13] Even now, the Bank was confi-

dently conducting backstairs negotiations with Secretary McLane to work out a formula for recharter, and it had inspired an effective press campaign to counteract Jackson's pronouncements. Benton, watching impatiently, concluded that someone (who else but Benton?) would have to set forth the hard-money case.

He tried several times to get the floor in the Senate, but the friends of the Bank succeeded always in silencing him by parliamentary technicalities. Finally, on February 2, 1831, he outmaneuvered the opposition and launched his comprehensive indictment: —

First: Mr. President, I object to the renewal of the charter . . . because I look upon the bank as an institution too great and powerful to be tolerated in a Government of free and equal laws. . . .
Secondly, I object . . . because its tendencies are dangerous and pernicious to the Government and the people. . . . It tends to aggravate the inequality of fortunes; to make the rich richer, and the poor poorer; to multiply nabobs and paupers. . . .
Thirdly, I object . . . on account of the exclusive privileges, and anti-republican monopoly, which it gives to the stockholders.

And his own policy? "Gold and silver is the best currency for a republic," he thundered; "it suits the men of middle property and the working people best; and if I was going to establish a working man's party, it should be on the basis of hard money; a hard money party against a paper party."[14] The words reverberated through the hall — "a hard money party against a paper party" — as Mr. Webster of Massachusetts hastily rose to call for a vote which defeated Benton's resolution against recharter.

13 Nicholas Biddle's statement in 1830 that opposition to recharter was "not . . . a cabinet measure, nor a party measure, but a personal measure" was accurate. Biddle to Samuel Smith, January 2, 1830, Biddle, *Correspondence,* R. C. McGrane, ed., 94. Few anticipated the emergence of the Bank as the crucial issue. Webster wrote to Clay on May 29, 1830, "The great ground of difference will be Tariff and Internal Improvements." Clay, *Private Correspondence,* Calvin Colton, ed., 276. Cf. Hezekiah Niles's comment on a letter by A. L. Dabney of Virginia: "His remark that it is the tariff and internal improvement policy that now divides the parties in the United States, is certainly true." *Niles' Register,* August 14, 1830. As late as 1831, Tocqueville was told repeatedly, among others by Biddle, that no real issues divided the parties. G. W. Pierson, *Tocqueville and Beaumont in America,* 49, 399, 495, 536. Tocqueville, who was a surprisingly poor political reporter, later incorporated this theory in his famous work.

14 Benton in the Senate, February 2, 1831, *Register of Debates,* 21 Congress 2 Session, 50–75; Benton, *Thirty Years' View,* I, 187–205.

But the words also reverberated through the country. The *Globe* speedily reprinted the speech, the party press took it up, and pamphlets carried it through the land, to be read excitedly by oil lamp and candlelight, talked over heatedly in taverns and around fireplaces, on steamboats and stagecoaches, along the crooked ways of Boston and the busy streets of New York and on isolated farms in New Hampshire, Missouri, Iowa, Michigan, Arkansas. Nathaniel Macon read it with deep pleasure in North Carolina. "You deserve the thanks of every man, who lives by the sweat of his face," he told Benton, adding with sturdy candor, ". . . I observe some bad grammar, — you must pardon my freedom."[15]

4

Nicholas Biddle, in his fine offices on Chestnut Street, was disturbed by much more than Benton's grammar. This able, suave and cosmopolitan Philadelphian was only thirty-seven when he became president of the Bank in 1823. He had been known mainly as a literary man — an early training which instilled a weakness for writing public letters that would often prove embarrassing. One English traveler pronounced him "the most perfect specimen of an American gentleman that I had yet seen" and commended his "exemption from national characteristics."[16]

As head of the Bank, he inclined to pursue an active policy; but up to 1830 all his ventures had succeeded, he had taken no unnecessary risks (except perhaps for the "branch draft" device), and his judgment was universally respected. Yet, for all his ability, he suffered from

a fatal self-confidence, a disposition to underrate his opponents and a lack of political imagination. He sought now to make a deal with the administration, while working on public opinion by newspaper articles, loans to editors and personal contacts. But his ultimate reliance was on two of the nation's giants, Henry Clay and Daniel Webster.

Henry Clay was the most beloved politician of the day. He was tall and a little stooped, with a sandy complexion, gray, twinkling eyes, and a sardonic and somewhat sensual mouth, cut straight across the face. In conversation he was swift and sparkling, full of anecdote and swearing freely. Reclining lazily on a sofa, surrounded by friends, snuffbox in hand, he would talk on for hours with a long, drawling intonation and significant taps on the snuffbox as he cracked his jokes. John Quincy Adams called him only half-educated, but added, "His school has been the world, and in that he is a proficient. His morals, public and private, are loose, but he has all the virtues indispensable to a popular man."

Brilliant, reckless, fascinating, indolent, Clay was irresistibly attractive. Exhilarated by his sense of personal power, he loved to dominate his human environment everywhere, in Congress and at party councils, at dinner and in conversation; but he was not meanly ambitious. If he possessed few settled principles and small analytical curiosity, he had broad and exciting visions, which took the place of ideas.

It was these rapt visions which made him so thrilling an orator. His rich and musical voice could make drama out of a motion for adjournment, and Clay took care that it ordinarily had much more to occupy itself with. His brilliance of gesture — the sharp nods of the head, the stamp of the foot, the pointed finger, the open palm, the tight-clenched fist — made

15 Macon to Benton, March 7, 1831, *Washington Globe*, June 17, 1831.

16 J. S. Buckingham, *America, Historical, Statistic, and Descriptive*, II. 214.

the emotion visible as well as audible. He carried all, not by logic, not by knowledge, but by storm, by charm and courage and fire. His rhetoric was often tasteless and inflated, his matter often inconsequential. "The time is fast approaching," someone remarked in 1843, "when the wonder will be as great, how his speeches could have been so thrilling, as it now is, how Mr. Burke's could have been so dull." Yet he transfixed the American imagination as few public figures ever have. The country may not have trusted him, but it loved him.[17]

Daniel Webster lacked precisely that talent for stirring the popular imagination. He was an awe-inspiring figure, solid as granite, with strong shoulders and an iron frame. His dark, craggy head was unforgettable; strangers always recognized the jet-black hair, the jutting brow, the large smoldering eyes, and the "mastiff-mouth," as Carlyle saw it, "accurately closed." Yet, he inclined to be taciturn in public, except when he worked up, with the aid of brandy, a heavy geniality for social purposes. He loved his comfort too much: liquor and rest, duck-shooting at Marshfield and adulation in Boston. His intellectual ability was great, but he used it only

under the spur of crisis. In his great speeches inspiration would take charge of his deep booming voice, and he would shake the world. Then he was, as Emerson remembered him, "the great cannon loaded to the lips." But when inspiration lagged he became simply pompous.

The nation never gave its heart to Webster. The merchants of Boston did, along with a share of their purses, and also the speculators of Wall Street and rich men everywhere. But the plain man did not much respond to him, except for a few Yankee farmers in New Hampshire, who liked to hobnob with statesmen. "He gives the idea of great power," said one English observer, "but does not inspire 'abandon.'" The people, who trusted Jackson and loved Clay, could neither trust nor love Webster. He never won the people simply because he never gave himself to them. He had, as Francis Lieber said, "no instinct for the massive movements."

Clay fought for Biddle and his Bank because it fitted in with his superb vision of America, but Webster fought for it in great part because it was a dependable source of private revenue. "I believe my retainer has not been renewed or *refreshed* as usual," he wrote at one point when the Bank had its back to the wall. "If it be wished that my relation to the Bank should be continued, it may be well to send me the usual retainers." How could Daniel Webster expect the American people to follow him through hell and high water when he would not lead unless someone made up a purse for him?[18]

In the House, Biddle could count on aid almost as formidable. John Quincy Adams, the ex-President, had come out of retirement to defend the American Sys-

[17] The quotations are from Adams, *Memoirs*, V, 325, and "Mr. Clay and the Restrictive System," *Democratic Review*, XII, 302 (March, 1843). See also G. W. Bungay, *Off-hand Takings; or, Crayon Sketches of the Noticeable Men of Our Age*, 21–24; T. C. Grattan, *Civilized America*, I, 172, II, 395–396; H. W. Hilliard, *Politics and Pen Pictures*, 3; C. C. Baldwin, *Diary of Christopher C. Baldwin, 1829–35*, 244; Martineau, *Retrospect*, I, 242, 275, 290; Lord Morpeth, Diary, manuscript transcript, 128, 141; "A Peep at Washington," *Knickerbocker Magazine*, III, 443 (June, 1834). I am also indebted to Leonard Woolf's brilliant sketch of Brougham for some suggestions on the interpretation of Clay: *After the Deluge*, II, 122. The resemblance between Clay and Brougham was noted by English visitors; see Tyrone Power, *Impressions of America, during the Years 1833, 1834, and 1835*, I, 270.

[18] The quotations are from Carlyle to Emerson, June 24, 1839, *Correspondence of Thomas Carlyle and Ralph Waldo Emerson, 1834–1872*,

tem in this moment of its peril. Adams, as Emerson noted, was no gentleman of the old school, "but a bruiser . . . an old roué who cannot live on slops but must have sulphuric acid in his tea!" He loved the rough-and-tumble of debate and neither asked quarter nor gave any. Sometimes he would lash himself into a rage, his body swaying with anger, his voice breaking, and the top of his head, usually white as alabaster, flushing a passionate red. Old age made him majestic and terrifying, with that bald and noble head, the cracked voice, the heavy figure clad in a faded frock coat. "Alone, unspoken to, unconsulted, never consulting with others, he sits apart, wrapped in his reveries," reported a Washington correspondent in 1837, ". . . looks enfeebled, but yet he is never tired; worn out, but ever ready for combat; melancholy, but let a witty thing fall from any member, and that old man's face is wreathed in smiles."[19]

Adams's protégé, Edward Everett, the great rhetorician, could also be relied on to embellish Biddle's case with splendid exordiums and perorations; and George

McDuffie, an experienced politician from South Carolina, was entrusted with the actual charge of the bill in the House. To strengthen the Bank forces, Biddle induced Horace Binney, the noted Philadelphia lawyer, to run for Congress. Binney had served as Bank lobbyist in Washington in the spring of 1832, and the next year took his seat as legislator.

In Clay, Webster, Adams, Everett, McDuffie and Binney, Biddle had a team whose personal following, abilities and oratory promised to overwhelm the best efforts of the administration. As the skirmishes began, he might be pardoned if he failed to regard Jackson, Benton and the Kitchen Cabinet as constituting a serious threat.

5

In the spring of 1830 a House committee, directed by George McDuffie, had brought in a report clearing the Bank of the charges made by Jackson in his first message to Congress. Jackson returned to the subject in more detail in his second message, and Benton's speech in 1831 thrust the question vigorously to the fore.

Biddle would have much preferred to keep the Bank out of politics altogether. His one interest was in renewing the charter. This he would do with Jackson's help, if possible; with Clay's, if necessary. Thus, during 1830 and 1831 he carefully explored the chances of winning over the President. The active co-operation of McLane and Livingston and the evident division in Jackson's party raised Biddle's hopes. The President, in the meantime, while saying quietly that his views had not changed, allowed McLane to recom-

---

C. E. Norton, ed., I, 247–248; R. W. Emerson, *Journals*, E. W. Emerson and W. E. Forbes, eds., VII, 87; Lord Morpeth, Diary, manuscript transcript, 102; Lieber to G. S. Hillard, December, 1852, T. S. Perry, *Life and Letters of Francis Lieber*, 256; Webster to Biddle, December 21, 1833, Biddle, *Correspondence*, 218.

Stephen Vincent Benét's recent skillful attempt to make Webster a hero of myth would have surprised many of Webster's contemporaries. The real Webster lacked the generosity and warm humanity of Mr. Benét's hero, and would have opposed many of the things which Mr. Benét himself has stood for today. In fact, the least plausible part of Mr. Benét's charming tale is not that a New Hampshire man should sell his soul to the devil, or that Benedict Arnold and Simon Girty should be on tap for jury service, but that Daniel Webster should be found arguing against the sanctity of contract.

[19] The quotations are from Emerson, *Journals*, VI, 349, and "Glances at Congress," *Democratic*

Review, I, 78–79 (October, 1837). See also "A Peep at Washington," *Knickerbocker Magazine*, III, 440 (June, 1834); John Fairfield to his wife, December 31, 1835, Fairfield, *Letters*, 47.

mend recharter in his Treasury report and barely mentioned the Bank question in his message of 1831.

But for all his amiability Jackson remained unyielding, while the Van Buren group seemed irrevocably hostile. Henry Clay, fearful lest so good an issue slip through his fingers, kept pressing Biddle to let him make recharter a party question. Biddle hesitated, considered, stalled, watched the National Republican convention nominate Clay, with John Sergeant, a lawyer for the Bank, as running mate, read the party address denouncing Jackson's views on the Bank — and on January 9, 1832, petitions for recharter were presented in each House of Congress.[20]

Benton, certain that the Bank could carry Congress, realized that the administration's only hope lay in postponement. Accordingly he had a good many obstructionist amendments prepared for the Senate, and in the House he set in motion plans for an investigating committee. Late in February, A. S. Clayton of Georgia moved the appointment of such a committee, defending the proposal from unexpectedly hot attacks by reading from hasty notes provided by Benton, twisting the paper around his finger so that no one would recognize the handwriting.[21]

The Bank forces could hardly refuse this request without raising strange suspicions. Yet, they first resisted it, then tried to keep it in their own hands, then tried to restrict its scope — overruling McDuffie who understood perfectly the futility of these tactics — with the result that by the time the committee was appointed the Bank had lost considerable prestige through the country. McDuffie,

[20] The best account of the Bank War is in Swisher, *Taney*, 160–326.

[21] Benton, *Thirty Years' View*, I, 232–241.

John Quincy Adams and J. G. Watmough, Biddle's vestpocket representative, served on the committee as friends of the Bank, with Cambreleng, Clayton, Richard M. Johnson and Francis Thomas of Maryland as opponents. After six weeks in Philadelphia, examining records and questioning witnesses, it issued three reports: a majority report against the Bank, and two minority dissents, one by Adams.[22]

In May the fight began in earnest. Biddle had already sent an advance guard of crack lobbyists, but, with the crucial struggle about to start, he took personal command. By now he was growing drunk with power. When Nathan Appleton, Massachusetts mill

[22] The operations of this committee confound naïve theories of economic determinism. All the opponents of the Bank were in debt to it (Clayton, $400; Johnson, $650; Thomas, $650; Cambreleng, $400), while the friends of the Bank owed it much less (McDuffie, $500; Watmough, $300; Adams, nothing). Though the Jacksonians made a good deal of the Bank's loans to Congressmen, there was not much correlation between the size of the loans and the intensity of the devotion to the Bank; see *House Report*, 22 Congress 1 Session, no. 460, "Bank of the United States," especially 569–570.

This statement does not apply at all, however, to loans to newspaper editors; and Taney's analysis of one Congressman's change of opinion after a large loan was certainly true for a small number of individual cases. "Now I do not mean to say," wrote Taney, "that he was directly bribed to give this vote. From the character he sustained and from what I knew of him I think he would have resented any thing that he regarded as an attempt to corrupt him. But he wanted the money — and felt grateful for the favor: and perhaps he thought that an institution which was so useful to him, and had behaved with so much kindness, could not be injurious or dangerous to the public, and that it would be as well to continue it. Men under the influence of interest or passion . . . do not always acknowledge even to themselves the motives upon which they really act. They sometimes persuade themselves that they are acting, on a motive consistent with their own self-respect, and sense of right, and shut their eyes to the one which in fact governs their conduct." Bank War Manuscript, 113–114.

owner and member of the House, proposed the charter be modified, Biddle scorned the suggestion, and Clay interceded with Appleton, begging him to vote for the measure as it stood. "Should Jackson veto it," exclaimed Clay with an oath, "I shall veto him!"[23]

[23] Robert C. Winthrop, "Memoir of Hon. Nathan Appleton," *Proceedings of the Massachusetts Historical Society*, V, 279.

On June 11 the bill passed the Senate, 28–20, and on July 3 it passed the House, 107–85. When Biddle made a smiling appearance on the floor after the passage, members crowded round to shake his hand. A riotous party in his lodgings celebrated the victory late into the night.[24]

[24] Taney, Bank War Manuscript, 116.

VETO

JESSIE BENTON knew she must keep still and not fidget or squirm, even when General Jackson twisted his fingers too tightly in her curls. The old man, who loved children, liked to have Benton bring his enchanting daughter to the White House. Jessie, clinging to her father's hand, trying to match his strides, would climb breathlessly up the long stairs to the upper room where, with sunshine flooding in through tall south windows, they would find the General in his big rocking chair close to the roaring wood fire. The child instinctively responded to the lonely old man's desire for "a bright unconscious affectionate little life near him," and would sit by his side while his hand rested on her head. Sometimes, in the heat of discussion, his long bony fingers took a grip that made Jessie look at her father but give no other sign. Soon Benton would contrive to send her off to play with the children of Andrew Jackson Donelson, the President's private secretary. Then the talk would resume. In the latter days of 1831 the discussions grew particularly long and tense.[1]

1

Jackson's grim calm during that year cloaked no basic wavering of purpose.

[1] Jessie Benton Frémont, *Souvenirs*, 88–89.

With characteristic political tact he presented an irresolute and amenable face to the world in order to hold the party together.[2] Benton and Kendall were in his confidence, but very few others. His apparent moderation deceived not only Biddle but many of the Bank's enemies. James A. Hamilton considered making a hurried trip to London to discuss Jackson's vacillations with Van Buren; and William Dunlap, the artist, voiced the misgivings of many liberals in his remark to Fenimore Cooper that Jackson had "proved weaker than could have been anticipated; yet those who hold under him will hold to him and strive to hold him up."[3]

In particular, Jackson's cabinet misinterpreted his pose. McLane, Livingston and Taney were all convinced that compromise was possible, greatly to the relief of the two and the despair of the third. Taney was coming to believe that he stood alone in the cabinet and almost in the country in opposing recharter. In the meantime, the Bank's alacrity in opening new offices and making long-

[2] The evidence for this view is set forth in Bassett, *Jackson*, 610–616.

[3] Bassett, *Jackson*, 612; Dunlap to Cooper, September 20, 1831, J. F. Cooper, *Correspondence*, J. F. Cooper, ed., I, 241.

term loans, though its charter was soon to expire, seemed "conclusive evidence of its determination to fasten itself by means of its money so firmly on the country that it will be impossible . . . to shake it off without producing the most severe and extensive public suffering. — And this very attempt," he cried, "calls for prompt resistance — for future resistance will be in vain if the charter is renewed."[4]

But who would lead the resistance? He watched the debates drag on and the votes pile up through the spring of 1832 with mounting apprehension. In the late spring, having to attend the Maryland Court of Appeals, he decided to prepare a memorandum setting forth his conviction that recharter should be vetoed. He finished it the night before his departure and notified the President that the opinion would be delivered as soon as the bill was passed.

On July 3 Jackson received the bill. Hearing the news, Martin Van Buren, just back from England, went straight on to Washington, arriving at midnight. The General, still awake, stretched on a sickbed, pale and haggard and propped up by pillows, grasped his friend's hand. Passing his other hand through his snow-white hair, he said firmly but without passion, "The bank, Mr. Van Buren, is trying to kill me, *but I will kill it!*"[5]

A day or two later, Taney, busy in Annapolis, received word to hurry back to Washington. He found the President out of bed and eager for action. He had read Taney's memorandum with emphatic agreement and then had heard the arguments of the rest of the cabinet. While disapproving the bill, they wanted

4 Taney to Thomas Ellicott, December 15, 23, 1831, Taney Papers; Taney, Bank War Manuscript, 104.

5 Van Buren, *Autobiography*, 625; *Political Parties*, 314.

him to place his rejection on grounds which would allow the question to be reopened in the future. Jackson, unwilling to compromise, then turned to Amos Kendall for a first draft of the veto message. Andrew J. Donelson was now revising Kendall's draft in the room across the hall. Would Taney help? The lean, determined face of the Attorney General expressed no reservations.

It took three days to finish the document. The first day Taney and Donelson worked alone, except for Jackson and Ralph Earl, an artist who lived at the White House and used this room as a studio, painting away, oblivious of the tense consultations, the hasty scribbles, the words crossed out, the phrases laboriously worked over, the notes torn up and discarded. On the second day Levi Woodbury, having decided to change his stand, made an unabashed appearance and assisted till the job was done. Jackson meanwhile passed in and out of the room, listening to the different parts, weighing the various suggestions and directing what should be inserted or altered.[6]

2

The message, dated July 10, burst like a thunderclap over the nation. Its core was a ringing statement of Jackson's belief in the essential rights of the common man. "It is to be regretted, that the rich and powerful too often bend the acts of government to their selfish purposes," Jackson declared. "Distinctions in society will always exist under every just government. Equality of talents, of education, or of wealth can not be produced by human institutions. In the full enjoyment of the gifts of Heaven and the fruits of superior industry, economy, and virtue, every man is equally entitled to protec-

6 Taney, Bank War Manuscript, 118–126.

tion by law; but when the laws undertake to add to these natural and just
advantages artificial distinctions . . . to
make the rich richer and the potent more
powerful, the humble members of society
— the farmers, mechanics, and laborers —
who have neither the time nor the means
of securing like favors to themselves,
have a right to complain of the injustice
of their Government."[7]

But the case against the Bank could
not rest simply on generalities. Jackson's
real opposition, of course, and that of
Benton, Taney and Kendall, arose from
their hard-money views. Yet, a great part
of their backing came from cheap-money
men. Thus powerful hard-money arguments — the economic argument that the
paper system caused periodic depressions, and the social argument that it
built up an aristocracy — were unavail-
able because they were as fatal to the
debtor and state banking positions as to
the Bank itself.

The veto message was brilliantly successful in meeting this dilemma. It di-
verted attention from the basic contra-
diction by its passages of resounding and
demagogic language; it played down the
strictly economic analysis; and it particularly sought to lull Western fears by
dwelling on the hardships worked by the
long arm of the Bank in the Mississippi
Valley. Its main emphasis fell, first, on
the case against the Bank as unconstitutional, and then on the political argument
that the Bank represented too great a
centralization of power under private
control. The stress on the "great evils to
our country and its institutions [which]
might flow from such a concentration of
power in the hands of a few men irresponsible to the people" sounded good
to the state banks and to the West, both
of which had chafed long enough at the

ascendancy of Chestnut Street.[8] The
message thus thrust to the foreground
the issues on which all enemies of the
Bank could unite, while the special aims
of the hard-money school remained
safely under cover.[9]

The distinction between "the humble
members of society" and "the rich and
powerful" drew quick reactions from
both classes. The common man through
the land responded enthusiastically to his
leader's appeal. "The veto works well
everywhere," Jackson could report from
the Hermitage in August; "it has put
down the Bank instead of prostrating
me."[10]

But men who believed that the political power of the business community
should increase with its wealth were
deeply alarmed. When Jackson said, "It
is not conceivable how the present stockholders can have any claim to the special
favor of the Government," did he mean
that the common man had the same
rights as the rich and wellborn to control of the state?[11] The Bank of the
United States, according to the plan of
Hamilton, would serve as the indispen-

[7] Richardson, comp., *Messages and Papers*, II,
590.

[8] Richardson, comp., *Messages and Papers*, II,
581.

[9] The Bank controversy elicited a few examples
of what would be a natural modern argument:
that the Bank was clothed with the public interest. Henry D. Gilpin, a former government director of the Bank and Attorney General under
Van Buren, suggested somewhat this argument
in 1836: "I am not sure that Dallas has put the
argument [against the bank] in its strongest form
— that such an institution is essentially *public*,
affecting the general value of property and exercising powers too broad to be regarded as private
acts — and that whether public or private the
chief legislative body have a right to rescind a
franchise, as they have to take private property,
when the public welfare requires it." Gilpin to
Van Buren, September 14, 1836, Van Buren
Papers.

[10] Jackson to W. B. Lewis, August 18, 1832,
Jackson–Lewis Letters.

[11] Richardson, comp., *Messages and Papers*, II,
577.

sable make-weight for property against the sway of numbers. Did not the veto message attack the very premises of Federalism, rejecting its axioms, destroying its keystone and rallying the groups in society bent on its annihilation?

No wonder Nicholas Biddle roared to Henry Clay, "It has all the fury of a chained panther, biting the bars of his cage. It is really a manifesto of anarchy, such as Marat or Robespierre might have issued to the mob of the Faubourg St. Antoine." Or, as Alexander H. Everett wrote in Boston's conservative daily, the *Advertiser*, "For the first time, perhaps, in the history of civilized communities, the Chief Magistrate of a great nation . . . is found appealing to the worst passions of the uninformed part of the people, and endeavoring to stir up the poor against the rich." Webster, rising gravely in the Senate, summed up the indictment: "It manifestly seeks to influence the poor against the rich. It wantonly attacks whole classes of the people, for the purpose of turning against them the prejudices and resentments of other classes. It is a State paper which finds no topic too exciting for its use, no passion too inflammable for its address and its solicitation." For Webster, as for Jackson, it was becoming a battle between antagonistic philosophies of government: one declaring, like Webster at the Massachusetts convention, that property should control the state; the other denying that property had a superior claim to governmental privileges and benefits.[12]

3

The veto struck consternation through some parts of the Democratic party. The summer and fall of 1832 saw a hasty re-

casting of party lines. In Boston, the ex-Federalist silk-stocking Democrats scurried back to their natural political allegiances, even at the cost of associating once again with John Quincy Adams. In New York, conservative politicians like G. V. Verplanck and businessmen like Moses H. Grinnell abandoned the radicals. Almost every city had its meeting of "original Jackson men" to disown the administration and renounce its works.

Two thirds of the press, largely perhaps because of advertising pressure, supported the Bank.[13] Even such a theoretically unpolitical family magazine as the *Saturday Evening Post* had opinions which led the *Washington Globe* to denounce it, in terms which would appeal to later generations, for conveying "its stealthy political influence into the bosom of such *families* as avoided the contests of politics."[14] Biddle also hired such august journals as Robert Walsh's *American Quarterly Review* to print pro-Bank articles.

13 Two thirds was the estimate of W. M. Holland in 1835, *Life and Political Opinions of Martin Van Buren*, 365; Van Buren's own estimate was three fourths, *Autobiography*, 746. As for the cause, as a discerning English traveler pointed out, "Relying chiefly, if not entirely, on their advertisements for support, and these being furnished by persons engaged in the mercantile and trading operations, they can hardly dare offend those on whom they are so dependent. . . . Hence they are almost all Whigs." Buckingham, *America*, III, 332. The report of the Philadelphia workingmen's committee of 1829, largely the work of two editors, W. M. Gouge and Condy Raguet, charged: "Even now it is impossible to obtain entrance into many papers for free disquisitions of the [banking] system. The conductor of a public journal who ventures on so bold a step, risks his means of subsistence." *Free Trade Advocate*, May 9, 16, 1829. Biddle's newspaper loans were notorious. The most celebrated example was the reversal of the policy of the *New York Courier and Enquirer*, formerly a strong Jackson paper, on receiving loans which aggregated to nearly $53,000 and were very risky business ventures.

12 Biddle to Clay, August 1, 1832, Clay, *Private Correspondence*, 341; A. H. Everett, *The Conduct of the Administration*, 60, 74–75; Webster in the Senate, July 11, 1832, *Register of Debates*, 22 Congress 1 Session, 1240.

14 *Washington Globe*, November 7, 1833.

A part of the business community stuck by Jackson. Some merchants opposed the concentration of power in the Bank. Some distrusted Biddle. Some hoped the Bank would be replaced by a Democratic Bank of the United States in which they might hold stock. Some were investors or officers in state banks with an eye on the government deposits. But they made up a small part of the whole. "Since landing in America," noted young Tocqueville, "I have practically acquired proof that all the enlightened classes are opposed to General Jackson."[15]

As the day of election drew near, the universal debate went on with increasing acrimony, from the shacks of Maine fishermen to the parlors of Philadelphia and the plantations of Alabama. An epidemic of cholera swept through the North in the first months of summer. "If it could only carry off Jackson and a few other of our politicians by trade," wrote Henry C. Carey, Philadelphia publisher and economist, "I would submit to all the inconveniences of it for a month or two." The din of politics, filling the cabin of a ship bound for America, wearied a charming British actress: "Oh, hang General Jackson!" cried Fanny Kemble.[16]

August gave way to September, September to October, and the clamor grew increasingly furious. Jackson men paraded the streets in the glare of torches, singing campaign songs, carrying hickory poles, gathering around huge bonfires blazing high into the night. Late in October, Horace Binney solemnly told a Philadelphia audience that "the preservation of the Constitution itself" depended on the defeat of Jackson, congratulating them that the right of a free election could still be exercised with safety. "How long it will continue so, or how long the enjoyment of it will be of any value to you, are questions upon which the short remainder of the present year will probably furnish materials for a decisive judgment." Fanny Kemble, resting in Philadelphia after her successes in Washington (where she had dazzled Chief Justice Marshall and Justice Story as well as Frank Blair of the *Globe*), was assured by her friends that Henry Clay, "the leader of the aristocratic party," was already certain of election.[17]

But the people had not spoken. Soon their time came: "The news from the voting States," Rufus Choate wrote to Edward Everett, "blows over us like a great cold storm."[18] The results rolled in: Jackson, 219, Clay, 49, John Floyd, 11, William Wirt, 7.[19] The bitterness with which conservatism faced the future flared up briefly in a post-election editorial in Joseph T. Buckingham's *Boston Courier*. "Yet there is one comfort left: God has promised that the days of the wicked shall be short; the wicked is old and feeble, and he may die before he

---

15 Pierson, *Tocqueville and Beaumont*, 484. For Tocqueville the "enlightened classes" were the merchants and lawyers, as Dr. Pierson points out, *ibid.*, 151.

16 Carey to J. F. Cooper, July 13, 1832, Cooper, *Correspondence*, I, 269; Parton, *Jackson*, I, v.

17 C. C. Binney, *Life of Horace Binney*, 98; Frances A. Kemble, *Records of a Girlhood*, 549.

18 Choate to Everett, November 10, 1832, Samuel G. Brown, *Life of Rufus Choate*, 61.

19 A later President's judgment on Jackson's opposition has bearing on both their experiences. "An overwhelming proportion of the material power of the Nation was against him. The great media for the dissemination of information and the molding of public opinion fought him. Haughty and sterile intellectualism opposed him. Musty reaction disapproved him. Hollow and outworn traditionalism shook a trembling finger at him. It seemed sometimes that all were against him — all but the people of the United States." Franklin D. Roosevelt, Jackson Day Address, January 8, 1936, *Public Papers and Addresses of Franklin D. Roosevelt*, Samuel I. Rosenman, ed., V, 40.

can be elected. It is the duty of every good Christian to pray to our Maker to have pity on us."[20]

4

Mr. McDuffie was addressing the House. He stammered, he shouted and screamed, he banged his desk and stamped the floor. The crowded galleries listened with fascination.

Sir, [a thump on desk upon a quire of paper heavy enough to echo over the whole hall] sir, South Carolina is oppressed, [a thump.] A tyrant majority sucks her life blood from her, [a dreadful thump]. Yes, sir, [a pause] yes, sir, a tyrant [a thump] majority unappeased, [arms aloft] unappeasable, [horrid scream] has persecuted and persecutes us, [a stamp on the floor.] We appeal to them, [low and quick,] but we appeal in vain, [loud and quick.] We turn to our brethren of the north, [low with a shaking of the head] and pray them to protect us, [a thump] but we t-u-r-n in v-a-i-n, [prolonged and a thump.] They heap coals of fire on our heads, [with immense rapidity] — they give us burden on burden; they tax us more and more [very rapid, slam-bang, slam — a hideous noise.] We turn to our brethren of the south, [slow with a solemn, thoughtful air.] We work with them; we fight with them; we vote with them; we petition with

them; [common voice and manner] but the tyrant majority has no ears, no eyes, no form, [quick] deaf, [long pause] sightless, [pause] inexorable, [slow, slow.] Despairing, [a thump] we resort to the rights [a pause] which God [a pause] and nature has given us, [thump, thump, thump]....[21]

They listened to more than just the ferocity of McDuffie: behind his hot periods raged the anger of a whole state, and behind his violent gesticulations stood the cold, consecrated figure of Calhoun, no longer Vice-President, now Senator from South Carolina. In July, 1832, Jackson had signed a new tariff bill, lowering the duties but leaving them still clearly protective. South Carolina, unsatisfied, prepared to object. The complex abstractions of the Exposition of 1828 were now seen to be tipped with steel, and nullification marched out of the study into the battlefield. Late in November, a state convention declared the tariffs of 1828 and 1832 void within the state after February 1, 1833.

Jackson met the South Carolina ordinance with a ringing proclamation on the nature of the Union, drawn up in large part by Edward Livingston. As the crisis approached, a "force bill," authorizing the President to use force to execute the laws, was introduced in the Senate. At the same time, however, the President acted to abate the actual grievance by furthering a compromise on the tariff. Late in December friends of Van Buren sponsored a much lower tariff bill in the House. Henry Clay, aware of the nation's peril but reluctant to enhance Van Buren's prestige or to reduce rates unduly, countered with a somewhat more protectionist compromise. By some parliamentary sleight-of-hand the Clay bill replaced the first bill in the House; and

[20] Reprinted in the *Washington Globe*, November 27, 1832. It continues in similar vein, declaring that the works of Paine "do not furnish Atheists with a single argument against the existence of a benign Providence, half so strong as the continuance of the misrule of Andrew Jackson. . . . We are constrained to acknowledge that the experiment of an absolutely liberal government has failed. . . . Heaven be praised that Massachusetts and Connecticut have escaped the moral and political contagion! As for the rest, they have proved themselves slaves, born to be commanded — they have put the whip into the hands of one who has shown every inclination to be absolute master, and it is some consolation to think that he will probably ere long lay it upon their backs till they howl again. . . . Who doubts that if all who are unable to read or write had been excluded from the polls, Andrew Jackson could not have been elected?"

[21] As seen by a correspondent for the *Portland Daily Advertiser*, reprinted in *Niles' Register*, August 17, 1833.

it also quickly passed the Senate with the support of Calhoun, who thought higher duties a small price to pay for the pleasure of thwarting Van Buren and the administration.

With compromise achieved, South Carolina now rescinded the ordinance nullifying the tariff, but, to score a final victory for its logic, it passed another, nullifying the now unnecessary force bill. This was a hollow triumph, for the episode had shown that in practice nullification was indistinguishable from rebellion and would call down the force of the government. Though nullification had paid its way this time, everyone knew it never would again.

By his masterly statesmanship Jackson had maintained the supremacy of the Union. But, in so doing, he had committed himself to doctrines on the nature of the Union which frightened the States'-rights fundamentalists among his supporters. The spectacle of Daniel Webster and John Quincy Adams defending Jackson in Congress, and of Justice Story remarking that he and Marshall had become the President's "warmest supporters," deepened Jeffersonian misgivings. Van Buren, ever cautious, was gravely concerned. C. C. Cambreleng objected to "the metaphysics of the Montesquieu of the Cabinet," as he labeled Livingston, but consoled himself that "happily the mass of the people sleep over such parts of it and dwell only on those which make them think and feel like men." Benton was without enthusiasm. Many years later, after guns had boomed over Sumter, Taney declared that he had not seen the proclamation until it was in print and that he disapproved some of its principles. Young Theodore Sedgwick, Jr., of Massachusetts asked the essential question: could Jeffersonians "endure from any other man the profession of the same sentiments which they received with ac-

clamation from General Jackson? Would these Doctrines be as safe in any other hands as they are in his?"[22]

Yet, only a few politicians and intellectuals worried about constitutional hairsplitting. The mass of the people, as Cambreleng observed, slept over such passages while responding unreservedly to the central appeal — the preservation of the Union. Party lines faded as men who had cursed Jackson a few months before now rushed to praise him. "It is amusing to witness the unanimity of public opinion at this moment," commented the popular novelist, Catharine Maria Sedgwick, " — to hear the old sober standard anti Jackson men, who tho't the republic was lost if he were reëlected say 'well: I really believe it is all for the best that Jackson is president.' "[23] It would not be the last time that conservatism, scared by national crisis, would shelter itself gratefully behind the vigorous leadership of a Democratic President it had previously denounced.

Jackson became for the moment the country's hero. It was whispered that even Daniel Webster, dissatisfied with a junior partnership in the opposition, would join the administration. Webster himself was reported to regard Jackson's anti-Bank attitude as the only obstacle — which led Louis McLane to remark, "I consider this only the last qualm of a frail lady, who notwithstanding, finally falls into the arms of the seducer." But why, in any case, should Jackson not forget the Bank? As McLane added, "if he devote the remainder of his term to tranquilize the public mind, he will go into

22 Story to Sarah Waldo Story, January 27, 1833, Story, *Story*, II, 119; Cambreleng to Van Buren, December 18, 1832, Van Buren Papers; Samuel Tyler, *Taney*, 189; Theodore Sedgwick, Jr., to Van Buren, January 22, 1833, Sedgwick Letterbooks.

23 Catharine M. Sedgwick to Theodore Sedgwick, January 20, 1833, Sedgwick Papers.

retirement with greater fame than any other man in our history."[24]

But these calculations omitted General Jackson, who cared less for his popularity than for his program. Early in December, Amos Kendall made one of his rare public speeches to the Central Hickory Club. "In all civilized as well as barbarous countries," he declared, "a few rich and intelligent men have built up *Nobility Systems;* by which, under some name, and by some contrivance, the few are enabled to live upon the labor of the many." These ruling classes, he said, have had many names — kings, lords, priests, fundholders, but all "are founded on deception, and maintained by power. The people are persuaded to permit their introduction, under the plea of public good and public necessity. As soon as they are firmly established, they turn upon the people, tax and control them by the influence of monopolies, the declamation of priestcraft and government-craft, and in the last resort by military force." Was America immune from this universal pattern? "The United States," said Kendall ominously, "have their young *Nobility System.* Its head is the Bank of the United States; its right arm, a protecting Tariff and Manufacturing Monopolies; its left, growing State debts and States incorporations."[25] The friends of Daniel Webster might well ponder these quiet words.

5

Jackson's re-election and the popular acclaim following the nullification crisis only reinforced the administration's resolve to press the offensive against the American "Nobility System." The first necessity was to destroy its "head," the Bank. But the charter still had well over three years to run. The Bank was still backed by the National Republican party, most of the press and many leading citizens. And the custody of the government deposits, the radicals feared, provided the Bank with campaign funds for recharter. Generous loans, subsidies and retainers, strategically distributed, might substantially change public opinion before 1836. Moreover, the government deposits, by enabling the Bank to take most of the specie out of circulation in exchange for its bank notes, might place Biddle in a position, just before the election of 1836, to create a financial panic and insure the success of Bank candidates and the recharter of the Bank.[26]

The solution lay in withdrawing the deposits. This would cripple the Bank's attempt to convulse the money market and probably provoke it into an all-out fight against the only man who could whip it, thus foreclosing the issue once and for all. Jackson seems to have decided on this course shortly after his re-election.[27] It was his own plan, "conceived by him," as Benton later wrote, "carried out by him, defended by him, and its fate dependent upon him."[28] Taney, Kendall and Blair actively supported him while Barry added his crumbling influence. Benton, vastly pleased, for some reason played little part in

---

[24] McLane to Buchanan, June 20, 1833, G. T. Curtis, *Life of James Buchanan,* I, 191–192.

[25] *Washington Globe,* December 13, 1832.

[26] Evidence of the Bank's intention to use its funds for political activity was marshaled by Taney in his "Report on the Removal of the Public Deposites," *Register of Debates,* 23 Congress I Session, Appendix, 66–67. For the fears of the radicals, see Kendall, *Autobiography,* 375; J. A. Hamilton to Jackson, February 28, 1833, Jackson, *Correspondence,* V, 22–23; Taney's speech of August 6, 1834, *Washington Globe,* August 25, 1834; Benton's speech of July 18, 1835, *ibid.,* August 8, 1835; etc.

[27] Marquis James effectively disposes of the story that Jackson believed the Bank insolvent, *Portrait of a President,* 334–335 and note.

[28] Benton, *Thirty Years' View,* I, 374.

working out the details. Woodbury remained inscrutable, with McLane, Livingston and Cass all hostile.

McLane and Biddle, indeed, went quickly to work to forestall the President. A special Treasury investigator reported early in 1833 that the Bank was sound, and in March the House upheld a majority report of the Ways and Means Committee declaring the funds perfectly safe in the Bank's custody. These incidents only confirmed the radicals' conviction of the extent of Biddle's power. The campaign for removal slowed down in May and June, during the President's trip to New York and New England. No overt act had yet destroyed his almost universal popularity, and the tour proved a long triumphal procession, marked by the thunder of cannon, the cheering of crowds, pompous reception committees and interminable banquets. General Jackson, though tormented by a throbbing pain in his side and the bleeding of his lungs, remained resolute and erect through it all.[29] . . . At Concord he finally collapsed and was hurried back to Washington.[30]

In the meantime the transfer of Livingston to the French ministry and of McLane to the State Department had created a vacancy in the Treasury for which McLane proposed William J. Duane, the Philadelphia lawyer who had signed the anti-Bank report of the working-men's meeting in March, 1829. Jackson approved, and Duane took office on June 1. This appointment raised fresh difficulties. Though Duane could hardly have been much surprised on learning Jackson's sentiments about removal, he played an equivocal part, neither accepting nor opposing the President's views,

but stalling and obstructing. Kendall and Reuben M. Whitney, another veteran of the workingmen's meeting in 1829, were working out the details of a system of deposit in selected state banks, and Duane finally agreed to resign if, after Kendall's report, he still found himself unable to take the desired action.

July, as usual, was unbearable in Washington. Jackson, sick and weary, prepared to go to Ripraps in Virginia for a rest. Where, in this moment of loneliness, stood the Vice-President? Van Buren at first had opposed immediate removal. The imminence of 1836, and his role as heir-apparent, had probably intensified his natural caution. Sometime in the spring, during a heated discussion with Van Buren, Amos Kendall, rising from his seat in excitement, warned that a Bank victory in 1836 was certain unless it were stripped of the power it gained from managing the public money: "I can live under a corrupt despotism, as well as any other man, by keeping out of its way, which I shall certainly do." Impressed by Kendall's vehemence, Van Buren changed his attitude, though he never allowed himself to become identified with the measure. His own private council, the Albany Regency, was divided, Silas Wright favoring delay, while A. C. Flagg and John A. Dix supported the President. During August and September Van Buren traveled around New York, first to Saratoga, then, with Washington Irving, taking a four-week tour of the Dutch settlements on Long Island and the North River, always one step ahead of the Washington mail. For once he was living up to his reputation.[31]

29 [A description of the tour is here omitted. — Ed.]

30 Josiah Quincy, *Figures of the Past*, 352 ff.

31 Kendall, *Autobiography*, 376; Hamilton, *Reminiscences*, 258; Van Buren, *Autobiography*, 601–604; correspondence between Jackson and Van Buren, August–September, 1833, Jackson, *Correspondence*, V; Silas Wright to Polk, January 21, 1845, R. H. Gillet, *Life and Times of Silas*

Frank Blair accompanied Jackson to the seaside, where the two households spent a pleasant month, the invigorating salt air restoring Jackson's appetite and improving his health. Letters bombarded the President, pleading with him not to disturb the deposits. What seemed an organized campaign only strengthened his purpose: "Mr. Blair, Providence may change me but it is not in the power of man to do it."[32] In spare moments, he shaped his notes into a militant and uncompromising document. Returned to the White House late in August, he resolved to end the matter before Congress convened.

On September 10 he presented Kendall's report on the state banks to the cabinet. Taney and Woodbury backed the proposal to discontinue placing funds with the Bank on October 1, while McLane, Cass and Duane vigorously opposed it. Duane's assent as Secretary of the Treasury was necessary for the action. By September 14 Jackson, having tortuously overcome his scruples against discharging persons who disagreed with him, suggested to Duane that he resign; perhaps he might be named Minister to Russia. Duane refused. The next day Jackson handed Taney for revision the fiery paper he had dictated at Ripraps. On the eighteenth he read this paper to the cabinet. Two days later the *Globe* announced the plan to cease deposits in the Bank after October 1. Duane continued in frightened obstinacy, agreeing to the removal of neither the deposits nor himself. "He is either the weakest mortal,

or the most strange composition I have ever met with," Jackson wrote in exasperation.[33] The next five days exhausted even the President's patience. He dismissed Duane and appointed Taney to the place.[34]

He now faced the threatened resignations of McLane and Cass. A friend of the Secretary of War told Blair that Cass would remain if a paragraph in the President's statement would exempt him from responsibility. Jackson, amused at the suggestion that Cass might be held responsible, said, "I am very willing to let the public know that I take the whole responsibility," and conceded the point. The amended message went off to the *Globe* for publication, and the next morning Blair took Taney the proofs. Taney, black cigar in mouth and feet on table, listened as Andrew J. Donelson read the message aloud. "How under heaven did that get in?" exclaimed Taney on hearing the inserted passage. When Blair explained, Taney observed, "This has saved Cass and McLane; but for it they would have gone out and have been ruined — as it is, they will remain and do us much mischief."[35]

The radical Jacksonians exulted at the removal. "This is the crowning glory of A. J.'s life and the most important service he has ever rendered his country," cried Nicholas P. Trist, the intelligent young Virginian who served as the President's secretary. "Independently of its misdeeds, the mere *power*, — the bare

Wright, II, 1644; Wright to Flagg, August 8, 1833, Flagg Papers (Wright added as another argument against removal the fear that "such men and mausers as Jas. A. Hamilton and Jesse Hoyt" might try to benefit in stock speculation by prior knowledge of removal).

52 Blair to Van Buren, November 13, 1859, Van Buren, *Autobiography*, 607.

33 Jackson to Van Buren, September 22, 1833, Jackson, *Correspondence*, V, 206.

34 Duane published in 1838 a plaintive defense of his odd behavior, called *Narrative and Correspondence Concerning the Removal of the Deposites*, and correctly described by the *New York Evening Post*, May 14, 1839, as a work of "feeble bitterness."

35 Blair to Van Buren, November 13, 1859, Van Buren, *Autobiography*, 608.

existence of such a power, — is a thing irreconcilable with the nature and spirit of our institutions." Benton pronounced it "the most masterly movement in politics which the age had witnessed." The *Boston Post* put it in the same class as Christ's expelling the money-changers from the Temple. The sturdy and rebellious William Cobbett, in England, called it "one of the greatest acts of his whole wonderful life." Jovial Charles

Gordon Greene, editor of the *Boston Post*, even composed an epitaph for the Bank: "BIDDLED, DIDDLED, and UNDONE."[36]

But Biddle was not yet convinced that it was the Bank which needed the epitaph.

[36] Trist to H. D. Gilpin, October 21, 1833, Gilpin Papers; Benton in the *Washington Globe*, August 8, 1835; *Boston Post*, October 15, 1833; William Cobbett, *Life of Andrew Jackson*, 120; *Boston Post*, October 18, 1833.

COUNTERATTACK

THE new storm of denunciation made the attack on the veto seem a model of good temper. Biddle, convinced by midsummer that the deposits were doomed, began in August to fight back. Employing to the full his power over the state banks, he commenced to present their notes for redemption, reduce discounts and call in loans. While claiming to be simply winding up business in preparation for the expiration of the charter, he was in fact embarked on the campaign the radicals above all had feared: the deliberate creation of a panic in order to blackmail the government into rechartering the Bank. "Nothing but the evidence of suffering abroad will produce any effect in Congress," he wrote privately to a friend. ". . . if . . . the Bank permits itself to be frightened or coaxed into any relaxation of its present measures, the relief will itself be cited as evidence that the measures of the Govt. are not injurious or oppressive, and the Bank will inevitably be prostrated." "My own course is decided," he informed another, " — all the other Banks and all the merchants may break, but the Bank of the United States shall not break."[1]

[1] Biddle to William Appleton, January 27, 1834, to J. G. Watmough, February 8, 1834, Biddle, *Correspondence*, 219, 221.

1

The strategy was at first brilliantly successful. The business community, already incensed by Jackson's measures, was easily persuaded that deflation was the inevitable consequence of removal. The contraction of loans by the Bank tightened credit all along the line. Businesses failed, men were thrown out of work, money was unobtainable. Memorials, petitions, letters, delegations and protests of every kind deluged Congress.

The friends of the administration now needed all their skill. Thomas Hart Benton still swaggered through the Capitol, a host in himself, and still rose to make his crushing speeches, pausing only to apply a double glass to his eye as he read the tedious, yet essential, statistics. But his footwork was slow, and the brunt of the defense in Senate debates fell rather on the shoulders of John Forsyth of Georgia, a good Southern politician, talented, facile and endowed with strong political loyalties which served him in place of principles. No one excelled Forsyth in the guerrilla aspects of debate, in reconnoitering and skirmishing, in leading the assault and covering the retreat.

In Isaac Hill of New Hampshire, Andrew Jackson had another firm defender.[2]. . . The special representative of Van Buren was Silas Wright, the Senator from New York. . . .[3]

2

Roger B. Taney set forth the issue in the report he rendered to the House early in the session. "It is a fixed principle of our political institutions," he declared, "to guard against the unnecessary accumulation of power over persons and property in any hands. And no hands are less worthy to be trusted with it than those of a moneyed corporation." What would be the future of American democracy if the course of the government was to be regulated by fear of the Bank? "They may now demand the possession of the public money, or the renewal of the charter; and if these objects are yielded to them from apprehensions of their power, or from the suffering which rapid curtailments on their part are inflicting on the community, what may they not next require? Will submission render such a corporation more forbearing in its course?"[4]

This was indeed the question: if Mr. Biddle's panic could coerce the Congress into restoring the deposits, would not the Bank, strengthened by the deposits, in the same manner coerce the Congress into recharter; and as its power grew, would not its demands become more exigent, until democracy was dead? "For, rely upon it," as Taney warned again in a speech in Maryland the next summer, "if the deposits are restored, the Bank is surely rechartered. And if, after all its

enormities, it obtains an extension of its charter for a single year, the contest is over, and we may quietly resign ourselves to the chains with which it is prepared to bind us."[5]

The Bank forces were now reinforced by the support, under complex and tenuous conditions, of John C. Calhoun. The philosopher from South Carolina proved helpful in lifting the issue to more elevated planes of discussion. He sharply denied that the struggle was over the question of Bank or no Bank. If it were, "if it involved the existence of the banking system, . . . I would hesitate, long hesitate, before I would be found under the banner of the system." What then was it all about? "I answer, it is a struggle between the executive and legislative departments of the Government; a struggle, not in relation to the existence of the bank, but which, Congress or the President, should have the power to create a bank, and the consequent control over the currency of the country. This is the real question."[6]

While this was hardly the real question, it was certainly a far nobler question than the discredited plea for recharter. It fitted neatly into the ancient picture of Jackson as a backwoods Caesar, bent on establishing a military dictatorship; and it supplied an issue on which the friends of the Bank and the friends of nullification could unite in an anti-Jackson front. Clay sounded the new keynote before a hushed Senate and packed galleries on the day after Christmas. "We are in the midst of a revolution," he declared, "hitherto bloodless, but rapidly tending towards a total change of the pure republican character of the Government, and to the concentration of all power in the hands of one

---

[2] [Cyrus P. Bradley], *Biography of Isaac Hill, passim;* B. P. Shillaber, "Experiences during Many Years," *New England Magazine,* VIII, 626 (July, 1893).

[3] [Descriptions of Hill and Wright are here omitted. — Ed.]

[4] Taney's report on the removal of the deposits, *Register of Debates,* 23 Congress 1 Session, Appendix, 68.

[5] *Washington Globe,* August 25, 1834.

[6] Calhoun in the Senate, January 13, 1834, *Register of Debates,* 23 Congress 1 Session, 217–218.

man." The currency had been undermined, the recharter vetoed against the will of the Congress, the system of internal improvements crushed, the tariff imperiled, and now liberty and the Constitution were themselves in danger. "If Congress do not apply an instantaneous and effective remedy, the fatal collapse will soon come on, and we shall die — ignobly die — base, mean, and abject slaves; the scorn and contempt of mankind; unpitied, unwept, unmourned!"[7]

Webster took up the attack, arguing the imminence of despotism with massive logic; Silas Wright replied, and Webster slashed back at Wright. (The two men disliked each other. Webster thought Wright "the most over-rated man" he had ever met, while Wright, regarding Webster as the Bank's henchman, had only contempt for his views "as far as he is competent to entertain views today which will govern his action tomorrow.")[8] For a moment in his rejoinder, Webster glanced from the fictitious issue to the real one. "Sir," he exclaimed, holding a newspaper clipping in his hand and turning his great, stern, dark face on Wright, "I see . . . plain declarations that the present controversy is but a strife between one part of the community and another. I hear it boasted as the unfailing security, the solid ground, never to be shaken, on which recent measures rest, that the poor naturally hate the rich." The great voice throbbed with indignation. Whoever was wicked enough thus to attack the Bank, "by arraying one class against another . . .

deserves to be marked especially as the poor man's curse!"[9]

But the Bank forces took care most of the time to avoid such issues, and the debates turned more and more on constitutionality. On February 5 a resolution passed declaring Taney's reasons for removal unsatisfactory, and on March 28 came another charging Jackson with having acted in derogation of the Constitution. When Jackson replied by a long protest, the Senate refused to enter it in its records, and the session came to a bitter end.

Events moved more favorably in the House. The quiet, remorseless leadership of James K. Polk kept the discussion to the point. "The Bank of the United States has set itself up as a great irresponsible rival power of the Government," he declared; and if it won this fight, no man thereafter could expect "to arrive at the first station in this great republic, without first making terms with the despot." He assailed the attempt to divert the debate into quibbles about constitutionality. "The present is, in substance and in fact, the question of recharter or no recharter. The question is, in fact, whether we shall have the republic without the bank, or the bank without the republic."[10]

Horace Binney replied in a three-day attack on the removal; but it was in terms of argument rather than invective, and Jackson, amiably inviting him to dinner, showed him, as Binney wrote back to an amazed Philadelphia, "a succession of the most obliging civilities, of the most marked and striking kind, from the beginning to the end of a really excellent

[7] Clay in the Senate, December 26–30, 1833, *Register of Debates*, 23 Congress 1 Session, 59–94.

[8] Peter Harvey, *Reminiscences of Webster*, 233; Wright to A. C. Flagg, January 31, 1836, Flagg Papers.

[9] Webster in the Senate, January 21, 1834, *Register of Debates*, 23 Congress 1 Session, 439–442.

[10] Polk in the House, January 2, 1834, *Register of Debates*, 23 Congress 1 Session, 2289.

dinner in every possible sense."[11] Cambreleng responded to Binney, and Samuel Beardsley, a rather conservative New York Democrat, added, in words which seemed to unveil the secret purposes of Jackson and Amos Kendall, that, if the credit and commerce of the country depended upon the Bank, "I, for one, say perish credit; perish commerce; . . . give us a broken, a deranged, and a worthless currency, rather than the ignoble and corrupting tyranny of an irresponsible corporation."[12]

Perish credit; perish commerce: these chilling words struck terror in the hearts of the more apprehensive conservatives. Was not this the whole drift of the administration policy? First, the Maysville veto, then the Bank veto, then the removal of the deposits — who knew what would follow? "How far this Catilinarian conspiracy has been carried, who but the miscreants concerned in the plot can now disclose to the nation?" snarled fiery Tristram Burges, of Rhode Island. "Have they already parcelled out our cities and villages, and appointed some Lentulus to superintend their conflagration?"[13] But Polk steered straight to his objectives, through all these furious gales, carrying through the House forthright resolutions against recharter, against restoration of the deposits, and in favor of a new deposit system employing state banks.

The President meanwhile remained unshaken by all the uproar. James Fenimore Cooper began to believe that "hickory will prove to be stronger than gold," and he need never have doubted. One day it was reported in Washington that a Baltimore mob was threatening to camp on Capitol Hill till the deposits were restored. A group of quaking administration Congressmen beseeched Jackson to say what was to be done. "Gentlemen," the old General reassured them with grim humor, "I shall be glad to see this federal mob on Capitol Hill. I will fix their heads on the iron palisades around the square to assist your deliberation. The leaders I will hang as high as Haman to deter forever all attempts to control the legislation of the Congress by intimidation and design."[14]

Delegations of businessmen, from New York, Baltimore and Philadelphia, also beset the President. Jackson, disliking to argue with people who were either fools enough to believe Nicholas Biddle or knaves enough to work for him, would make his unshakable determination clear by launching into fearful tirades against the Bank. A deputation from New York found him writing at his desk, smoking fiercely away at his long pipe. He excused himself, finished the paper and rose. "Now gentlemen, what is your pleasure with me?" James G. King, son of Rufus King, had hardly spoken a few sentences of a prepared address asking for relief when Jackson interrupted angrily: "Go to Nicholas Biddle. We have no money here, gentlemen. Biddle has all the money. He has millions of specie in his vaults, at this moment, lying idle, and yet you come to *me* to save you from breaking." And so on, with mounting vehemence, until the visitors departed. The man who had introduced them was

11 Binney to his son, January 10, 1834, Binney, *Binney*, 111.

12 Beardsley in the House, January 16, 1834, *Register of Debates*, 23 Congress 1 Session, 2450.

13 Burges in the House, March 26, 1834, *Register of Debates*, 23 Congress 1 Session, 3166.

14 Cooper to Dr. De Lancey, December 20, 1833, Cooper, *Correspondence*, I, 331; Blair to George Bancroft, June 24, 1845, Jackson, *Correspondence*, V, 238 n.

overtaken by a messenger on the White House stairs and asked to return to the President's office. He found Jackson chuckling over the interview: "Didn't I manage them well?"[15]

A Philadelphia delegation barely announced its mission when Jackson broke in with an excited speech. "*Andrew Jackson* never would restore the deposites to the bank — *Andrew Jackson* would never recharter that monster of corruption. . . . sooner than live in a country where such a power prevailed, he would seek an asylum in the wilds of Arabia." (Biddle, on hearing this, observed that he might "as well send at once and engage lodgings.") A Baltimore deputation, waiting on Taney, declared that, unless the government changed its policy, a large part of the business community would fail, and understood Taney to reply, "If *all* did fail, the policy of the government would not be changed." Jackson provided little more sympathy. "The failures that are now taking place," he told them, "are amongst the stock-jobbers, brokers, and gamblers, and would to God, they were all swept from the land!" *Go to Nicholas Biddle* was Jackson's refrain, until he felt that his interviews had been so deliberately misquoted that he would receive no more committees.[16]

"THE NATION STANDS ON THE VERY BRINK OF A HORRIBLE PRECIPICE," exclaimed Hezekiah Niles, in March, on behalf of the business community. A month later he announced with alarm that it is later than you think: "*Things cannot remain and stand still*. . . . Wives, children and property — liberty and peace — are the things which are under consideration. . . . A worse or better state must

soon happen." Fanny Kemble turned a moment from her army of admirers to note that everything threatened "change and disintegration." While playing "The Inconstant" in Philadelphia, she toasted "*Here's the deposites back again*" in one scene, and the audience roared its approval. Late in the summer another English lady, sharp-eyed, spinsterish and deaf, arrived in America. The first person Harriet Martineau met was quick to inform her that the nation was on the verge of a military despotism.[17]

The "natural aristocracy" was everywhere shocked into fantasies of collapse. Chancellor Kent departed from judicial calm to proclaim comprehensively: "I look upon Jackson as a detestable, ignorant, reckless, vain & malignant tyrant." Justice Story was sufficiently under the influence of Clay's rhetoric to observe, "Though we live under the form of a republic we are in fact under the absolute rule of a single man." He felt himself called back as in a dream to the last days of the Roman republic, when the mob shouted for Caesar, and liberty expired with the dark and prophetic words of Cicero. "It has been remarked with much justice and truth," a Missouri businessman wrote Frank Blair, "that the merchants through the United States, as a class, are opposed to our present Administration."[18]

On the very day that Story was delivering himself of his classical vision, Edward Everett told an English banker, "The present contest is nothing less than

15 Parton, *Jackson*, III, 549–550.

16 *Niles' Register*, March 1, 8, 15, 22, 1834; Biddle to Joseph Hopkinson, February 21, 1834, Biddle, *Correspondence*, 222.

17 *Niles' Register*, March 8, April 19, 1834; Frances A. Kemble, *Records of a Girlhood*, 568; *Boston Post*, March 22, 1834; Harriet Martineau, *Society in America*, I, 8.

18 Kent to Story, April 11, 1834, *Proceedings of the Massachusetts Historical Society*, xxxiv, 418; Story to S. P. Fay, February 18, 1834, Story, *Story*, II, 154; *Washington Globe*, December 5, 1834.

a war of Numbers against Property." He reported the rise of the mob with horror. "In Philadelphia, after the powerful expression of sentiment proceeding from the merchants and men of business, [Congressman] Southerland coolly observed that this was only the view of Chestnut Street and Market Street; that he went to the lanes and alleys, where they held a different language." Appalling — and only one man, Daniel Webster, could save the nation, though this, of course, required certain preliminaries! Everett was candid: "If our friends in Boston mean that their houses, their lands, their stocks shall really be their own much longer, they must make the effort; they must make it at once. It is but $1000 each for one hundred gentlemen."[19]

3

But Biddle could not hope to fool the business community indefinitely. More and more merchants were coming to believe that he was carrying the money pressure farther than necessary, and few would agree that it was worth breaking "all the other Banks and all the merchants" to restore Nicholas Biddle to power. Late in February, Governor George Wolf of Pennsylvania, hitherto a leading Bank Democrat, came out against the Bank. Clay probably sensed the reaction in March when Van Buren offered to bet him a suit of clothes on the elections in Virginia and New York City. The Senator responded gallantly that if the people did support the administration, he would fear self-government had failed; but it is noticeable that he did not take up the Vice-President's wager.[20]

In the same month, the leading merchants of Boston gathered at Faneuil Hall to appoint a committee to go to Washington with another petition. When Nathan Appleton, the chairman, reached New York, he discovered his old suspicion of Biddle's motives confirmed by James G. King and Albert Gallatin. King, as chairman of a New York committee, had already threatened the Bank with exposure if it did not change its policy. (*Go to Nicholas Biddle,* the old General had said; James G. King was quick to get the point.) Though Biddle had ignored earlier attempts at persuasion, this threat spoke in another tone, and he hurried to New York for personal consultations. Appleton and others of the Boston committee backed up King and Gallatin, informing Biddle that he knew very well the contraction was not necessary for the safety of the Bank, and that his whole object was to extort a charter from the government. Biddle could not talk himself out of the hole, and he knew that repudiation by Gallatin, an honored champion of the Bank, would be fatal. "Hence the Bank had to do something," as he explained to Watmough, the Bank lackey, "for the evil of such an announcement would have been enormous." So during April the pressure relaxed, but in May it resumed with greater violence than before, though even Webster now counseled prudence.[21]

On returning to Boston, Appleton found that, though the politicians proposed to support Biddle at any cost, the business community had lost all patience. When the contraction continued into June, he wrote a long letter to the direc-

[19] Everett to T. W. Ward, February 18, 1834, *Boston Herald,* February 24, 1913.

[20] Clay to Francis Brooke, March 23, 1834, Clay, *Private Correspondence,* 383.

[21] Appleton to George Ticknor, February 4, 1853, Appleton Papers; Winthrop, "Nathan Appleton," *Proceedings of the Massachusetts Historical Society,* V, 287–288; Biddle to Watmough, March 17, 1834, Catterall, *Second Bank,* 341.

tors of the Boston branch for transmission to Biddle. Signed by many of the solidest and most conservative merchants — such men as George Bond, Henry Lee, Warren Dutton, Amos Lawrence, G. W. Lyman, W. P. Eustis — and also approved by Abbott Lawrence and William Appleton, it abundantly documented the Jacksonian indictment from a quarter whose every predilection was on the side of Nicholas Biddle.

It is well understood that the Bank is pursuing a regular system of contraction apparently at the rate of about a million of Dollars per month, — the effects of which have been a renewal, since the first of May, of the pressure on the money market, and which threatens to Paralize business for the future, indefinitely, so long as it shall be continued. At the same time the Statement of the Bank for the month of June shows a degree of strength wholly unprecedented in the history of the Bank, and its ability, with perfect safety to itself, not merely to relieve the pressure, but to make discounts far beyond the present actual wants of the community. No satisfactory reason has been assigned for this course. It has sometimes been put forward, that it is necessary for the Bank, preparatory to wind up its concerns on the expiration of its charter — but however good a reason that may be for reducing the amount of pure accommodation loans, it cannot be considered any reason for refusing to employ its funds in discounting business paper in the commercial cities, or on the pledge of its own on other stocks. — It is not supposed that this ground of the necessity of this course preparatory to winding up its concerns, has been taken by the Bank, since if it were sound it would go far to justify the government, in the removal of the deposites. . . .

Under these circumstances it is not perhaps surprizing that public opinion, even amongst the most intelligent of our commercial men of the Whig Party, should attribute to the Bank the design, unnecessarily if not

wantonly to continue the pressure for the purpose of operating upon the fall elections. And it is quite apparent, that the general diffusion of this opinion, must operate most unfavourably upon the Bank, and in some measure upon the party which supports it. — It may even create a necessity for the Whigs in self-defence to separate themselves entirely from that institution. — In this state of things the subscribers are of opinion, that the interest of the Bank, of the country and of the party, requires a change of measures, and that no time should be lost in adopting it, as the only mode of averting a most dangerous crisis.

Biddle responded evasively and desperately, apparently even denying that there was any systematic curtailment of discounts. In a second letter Appleton blasted Biddle's claims with a grim array of evidence, mostly taken from the Bank's own statements, concluding with the harsh but essential question: "what is the policy of the Bank? why is it pursuing a course of policy so utterly irreconcilable with the ordinary principles of Banking?"[22]

4

Biddle acknowledged the answer himself on September 16 when he gave the lie direct to the case for curtailment by suddenly entering on a policy of expansion. After reducing its loans by well over

[22] Appleton, et al., to the Board of Directors of the United States Branch Bank at Boston (draft), June 21, 1834, Appleton to Biddle (draft), July, 2834, Appleton Papers. Appleton's opinion of Biddle did not improve with time. "The case of the U. States Bank," he wrote in 1853, ". . . was the result of Mr. Biddle's wanton abuse of the power intrusted to him. He pursued a course of unnecessary contraction under the pretence that it was necessary to the winding up of the Bank, until after the rising of Congress, when finding that he could not coerce them into renewal of the charter he most wantonly and recklessly increased his discounts." Appleton to Samuel Hooper, February 21, 1853, Appleton Papers; cf, Appleton, Remarks on Currency, 38–39.

eighteen million dollars from August 1, 1833, to November 1, 1834, under the plea of winding up its affairs, the Bank in the next five months *increased* its loans by almost fourteen and a half million. On June 1, 1835, the loans were almost what they were when Biddle's campaign began in August, 1833, and the note circulation was actually greater than ever before.[23] The panic was over, and the Bank had not recovered the deposits.

Somewhere along the way, Biddle had lost his grip on reality. Ambition, vanity and love of power had crossed the thin line to megalomania. So little had he understood the American people that he ordered the circulation of thirty thousand copies of the Bank veto as a campaign document for Henry Clay. He completely misconceived the grounds of the Jacksonian attack; and, when the President stated them, Biddle brushed the explanation aside as mere demagogy. As late as the summer of 1833, he still believed that Jackson's secret purpose was to found a new national bank of his own.[24]

Senator Theodore Frelinghuysen of New Jersey, his friend and defender, found the exact image for such a man. "There," Frelinghuysen observed with satisfaction, speaking on the effects of the panic, "sits Mr. Biddle, in the presidency of the Bank, as calm as a summer's morning, with his directors around him, receiving his salary, with everything moving on harmoniously: and has this stroke reached him? No, sir. The blow

has fallen on the friends of the President [Jackson] and the country." What a touching picture of innocent virtue! (Roger B. Taney muttered ungraciously, "Nero is said to have fiddled while Rome was burning, but I have not learned from history that even his courtiers praised him for doing so.")[25]

Biddle continued to console himself by fantasy. "My theory in regard to the present condition of the country is in a few words this," he wrote in 1835. "For the last few years the Executive power of the Govt. has been wielded by a mere gang of banditti. I know these people perfectly — keep the police on them constantly — and in my deliberate judgment, there is not on the face of the earth a more profligate crew." He warned the alumni of Princeton of the insolent ambitions of "some frontier Cataline." "It cannot be," he concluded with a flash of bravado, "that our free nation can long endure the vulgar dominion of ignorance and profligacy. You will live to see the laws re-established — these banditti will be scourged back to their caverns — the penitentiary will reclaim its fugitives in office, and the only remembrance which history will preserve of them, is the energy with which you resisted and defeated them."[26]

23 *Washington Globe*, April 13, June 10, 1835.

24 Catterall, *Second Bank*, 241; Biddle to J. S. Barbour, July 11, 1833, Biddle, *Correspondence*, 210.

25 Frelinghuysen in the Senate, January 27, 1834, *Congressional Globe*, 23 Congress 1 Session, 129; for variant version, see *Register of Debates*, 23 Congress 1 Session, 340; Taney, Bank War Manuscript, 29.

26 Biddle to Herman Cope, August 11, 1835, Biddle, *Correspondence*, 255; Biddle, *Address before the Alumni Association of Nassau Hall*, 22, 23.

HARD MONEY

THE determination which enabled Jackson to resist the hysteria of panic came basically from the possession of an alternative policy of his own. Madison had surrendered to a corresponding, though less intense, pressure in 1816 because he had no constructive program to offer. But, for Jackson, the emotions and ideas which underlay the hard-money case against the Bank were crystallizing into a coherent and concrete set of measures, designed to capture the government for "the humble members of society," as Hamilton's system had captured it for "the rich and powerful."

1

The Jeffersonian tradition provided the main inspiration for this program. The Virginia condemnation of paper money, pronounced by Jefferson, formulated profoundly by Taylor, kept pure and uncompromising by Macon and Randolph, had passed on as a vital ideological legacy to Jackson, Benton, Van Buren, Polk, Cambreleng. Yet it was handed down as a series of keen but despairing criticisms delivered in the shadow of an invincible industrialism. The creative statesmen of the Jackson administration now proposed to transform it into a positive governmental policy.

The Bank War played an indispensable role in the precipitation of hard-money ideas. It dramatized currency questions in a way which captured the imagination of the people and excited their desire for further action on the financial front. It enlisted the enthusiasm of intellectuals, stimulating them to further analysis, widening the range and competence of economic theory. It tightened class lines, and the new bitterness

of feeling sharpened the intellectual weapons.

Above all, the Bank War triumphantly established Jackson in the confidence of the people. Their faith in him had survived ordeals and won vindication: thereafter, when faced by a choice between Jackson and a cherished policy, most of them would choose Jackson. The effect of this mandate was particularly to sell the West on an intricate economic program, which many Westerners did not understand and which ran counter to their preconceptions.

The uncertainty about the West had postponed the avowal of the hard-money system.[1] The veto message, written by three men of known hard-money convictions, Jackson, Taney and Kendall, suppressed mention of the doctrine, as if by main force. But the election of 1832 increased Jackson's confidence. He could have lost the entire West and still have broken even with Clay, but he carried the whole West except for Kentucky.[2] He now felt certain of vigorous national support, and also of probable Western support, even for his economic ideas. Not all the West would follow, of course, and even three leaders from his own state turned against him on the currency question: his old friend Hugh Lawson White,

[1] Orestes A. Brownson later declared that he had been urged in 1831 by "men high in the confidence of the party ... to support the administration of that day, on the ground that it was opposed to all corporate banking, whether state or national." This was, of course, long before any such purpose was avowed as party policy. *Boston Reformer*, August 4, 1837.

[2] The "West" here includes Alabama, Mississippi, Louisiana, Kentucky, Tennessee, Ohio, Indiana, Illinois and Missouri. Jackson had only to carry one Western state to get a majority of the electoral votes.

young and able John Bell, and the picturesque if somewhat phony frontiers-
man, Davy Crockett. Others of his Western supporters, like Robert J. Walker of
Mississippi, were careful to disclaim any
hard-money leanings.[3] But, on the whole,
the magic of Jackson's name was fairly
certain to win Western approval for
almost anything.

He thus was emboldened to come out
publicly for the hard-money policy, expressing himself first in his interview
with the Philadelphia delegation a few
days before his second inaugural. His
objective, he said, was gradually to reduce the circulation of paper, by forbid-
ding deposit banks to issue small notes
and by refusing such notes in payment
for taxes, until all notes under twenty
dollars would be eliminated and "thus a
metallic currency be ensured for all the
common purposes of life, while the use
of bank notes would be confined to those
engaged in commerce."[4]

Soon after, he reorganized his cabinet,
turning it for the first time into an effective unit. McLane and Duane, both
evidently hostile to a radical economic
policy, were replaced by John Forsyth
in the State Department and Roger B.
Taney in the Treasury. William T. Barry,
whose incompetence as Postmaster General finally drove even Jackson to despair,
was succeeded by Amos Kendall. Benjamin F. Butler of New York, Van
Buren's former law partner, followed
Taney as Attorney General, and, after
Taney's eventual rejection by the Senate,
Levi Woodbury was promoted to the
Treasury. In this circle of staunch hard-
money men Lewis Cass could only re-
lapse into mournful silence. The administration was now streamlined for action.

2

The hard-money system owed many
of its maxims and dogmas to the Jeffersonians, and much of its vitality to the
Northern workingmen who backed it so
warmly; but the man to whom, after
Jackson, Benton and Taney, it perhaps
owed most for its emergence as a constructive policy was William M. Gouge,
the Philadelphia editor and economist.
Gouge put the hard-money doctrines in
the clearest form, furnished the most
cogent indictment of the paper system,
stated the general problems in a way
(unlike the Jeffersonian) relevant to a
society where finance capitalism was well
entrenched, and proved unfailingly re-
sourceful in working out the practical
measures to realize his policy. Thirty-
seven years old in 1833, he had been
from 1823 to 1831 editor and part proprietor of the *Philadelphia Gazette*. For
the next two years, he busied himself
with a treatise on the banking system,
published in Philadelphia in February,

[3] "God save us from the wild, visionary, ruinous,
and impractical schemes of the senator of Missouri," Walker cried in 1837. ". . . Sir, in resistance to the power of the Bank of the United
States, in opposition to the re-establishment of
any similar institution, the Senator from Missouri would find Mr. W. with him; but he could
not enlist as a recruit in this new crusade against
the banks of his own and every other State in the
Union. . . . [It] was not, he believed, anticipated
by any one of his constituents." Walker in the
Senate, January 28, 1837, *Register of Debates*,
24 Congress 2 Session, 621–622. Note Walker's
emphasis on "resistance to the power of the
Bank" as his main motive in fighting it. In 1840,
when Walker, now a strong hard-money man,
undertook to explain the origins of the hard-
money policy, he correctly declared: "The workingmen of the city of New York, next, perhaps
to the patriot Jackson and the Senator from Missouri, may be justly considered the original Loco
Focos and hard money men of the Union."
Walker in the Senate, January 21, 1840, *Congressional Globe*, 26 Congress 1 Session, Appendix, 140.

[4] *Niles' Register*, March 1, 1834.

1833, under the title *A Short History of Paper Money and Banking in the United States.*[5]

The work consisted of an analysis of the social consequences of the paper system, followed by a detailed account of the history of paper money in America. The first section set forth the broad theoretical case, while the second provided the crushing documentation. Facts were Gouge's most powerful weapons; and in a plain, circumstantial way, occasionally flavored by irony, constantly buttressed by names, dates and citations, he supplied a crisp and comprehensive statement of the hard-money position.

The book became an instant success. Probably no work in economics had ever circulated so widely in the United States. The first edition was nearly exhausted by the fall of 1834, and, in 1835, it was reprinted in cheap stereotyped form to sell for twenty-five cents. By 1837 it had gone into a third edition. It was serialized in the *New York Evening Post* in 1834, and later in the *Washington Globe* and many other papers, William Cobbett published an English edition, and an abridged version was translated into French and printed at Brussels. All the radicals of the day read it voraciously — William Leggett, Theophilus Fisk, Orestes A. Brownson, William Cullen Bryant — and paid cordial tribute to the author. It delighted Frank Blair, was passed from hand to hand in the inner circle of the government; and early in 1835 Gouge was called down to Washington to take a job under Levi Woodbury in the Treasury Department. There his terse and hard-hitting memoranda were to exert for many years an important influence on financial policy.[6]

The book's success was deserved. Its historical sections went unchallenged, even by the most ardent defenders of the system; and Gouge's keenness of analysis, as well as his accuracy, has won the approval of our ablest historians of banking. When it was first published Condy Raguet called it "decidedly the best work on Banking that we have ever met with." Modern students have treated it with similar respect. As William Graham Sumner, no friend of Jacksonian democracy, put it, Gouge "studied this system [of paper money] in its operation more thoroughly and with more intelligence than anybody else." A popular jingle expressed contemporary appreciation: —

Of modern books, the best I know —
    The author all the world is thanking —
One written more for use than show,
    Is quaintly titled, "*Gouge* on Banking."

But still improvements might be made,
    Whilst books on books the world is
        scrouging,
Let *Biddle* try to help the trade,
    And write one titled, "Banks on
        Gouging."[7]

3

The hard-money policy was conceived by Gouge and its other champions as a total alternative to the Hamiltonian system. Its central point was the exclusion

---

[5] Gouge's own copy, with interleaved notes, is in the Harvard College Library.

[6] *Journal of Banking*, July 7, 1841; *New York Evening Post*, September 15, 1834, June 29, 1837.

[7] *The Examiner, and Journal of Political Economy*, October 30, 1833; W. G. Sumner, *History of Banking in the United States*, 181; *Journal of Banking*, August 18, 1841. The leading modern historian of early banking theories remarks: "Gouge was one of the most thorough students of our early banking and also one of its keenest and most influential critics." Miller, *Banking Theories in the United States before 1860*, 86 n. For Nicholas Biddle's characteristic misjudgment of Gouge's work and its significance, see Biddle to J. S. Barbour, July 11, 1833, Biddle, *Correspondence*, 211. For the impact of Gouge on an ordinary intelligent and untutored young man, see Lucian Minor, "Diary of a Journey to the West in 1836," *Proceedings of the Massachusetts Historical Society*, XXVII, 284, 286.

of banks from control over the currency. It was not, as its opponents persisted in describing it, a demand for the annihilation of the banking system and the establishment of an exclusively metallic currency. It proposed merely to limit bank paper to commercial transactions, and to confine banks to the functions of deposit and discount, slowly withdrawing from them the privilege of note issue.[8]

The main purposes were three. One was essentially economic: to prevent periodic depressions; another essentially political: to prevent the rise within the state of independent powers, not responsible to the people and able to defy the government; and the third essentially social: to prevent the rule of a moneyed aristocracy systematically exploiting the "humble members of society."

The economic argument was brought to public attention largely by Benton and Gouge, and it drew somewhat on the reports of the English bullionists. The political was, of course, central in the American tradition; it was perhaps the particular contribution of the frontier to this controversy, and had been thrust forward during the Kentucky Relief War. The social argument represented the Jeffersonian legacy and was indebted considerably in its details to John Taylor of Caroline. As political expediency dictated, one could be stressed at certain times and others concealed. The Bank veto, for example, confined itself mainly to the second argument, with some suggestions of the third. But, after the election of 1832 had demonstrated the national confidence in Jackson, the administration began to urge all three. Gouge's book stated them conveniently, and Jackson's Farewell Address provided an excellent brief summary.

The economic argument turned ultimately on varying attitudes toward the concrete economy as an environment for living, rather than on disagreement over abstract principles. Alexander Hamilton in his eagerness to make out a case for paper money had once argued that note issue constituted "an absolute increase of capital," but this obviously untenable view was pretty well abandoned by 1830.[9] Even the most fervent admirers of paper money acknowledged the value of increasing the proportion of specie in the circulating medium. Nicholas Biddle himself in some moods was a hard-money man.[10] Daniel Webster loudly and constantly proclaimed the evils of overissue, except when he had to vote on a measure intended to prevent it.

Yet men like Biddle and Webster plainly preferred in last analysis a speculative economy, with quick expansion, huge gains and huge risks. During the investigation of the Bank by the Clayton Committee, when Cambreleng asked whether the existing banking system did not encourage speculation, Biddle replied: "Until the nature of man is changed, men will become speculators and bankrupts — under any system — and I do not perceive that our own is specially calculated to create them." Cambreleng became more specific. Would not the system be more healthy if note issue were forbidden? Biddle hedged: "I fear I do not comprehend all this. . . . That banks do occasional mischief there can

[8] See Appendix.

[9] Miller, *Banking Theories,* 30–34.

[10] In 1832 Biddle recommended the following reforms: "First, to widen the basis of the metallic circulation, by abolishing the use of small notes. . . . And second, to annex to the non-payment of specie by the banks, so heavy a penalty . . . as would deprive the banks of all temptation to incur the risk of insolvency." *House Report,* 22 Congress 1 Session, no. 460, "Bank of the United States," 367. For a typical expression of a theoretical preference for hard money hedged round by practical arguments against it, see Edward Everett, "Address to the Legislature," Massachusetts *House Document,* no. 6 (1836), 16–18.

be no doubt; but until some valuable improvement is found which supplies unmixed good, this is no objection to them. And constituted as they now are, the banks of the United States may be considered safe instruments of commerce."[11]

Biddle and men like him were willing to take the chance of depression in exchange for the thrills and opportunities of boom. But others confronted a speculative situation with much less confidence. Men of small and fairly fixed income — farmers, laborers, mechanics, petty shopkeepers, many of the Southern planters — felt themselves the victims of baffling and malevolent economic forces which they could not profit by or control.

On the most obvious level, the working classes believed that they were regularly cheated by paper money. A good portion of the small notes they received in wages were depreciated, worthless or counterfeit. Unscrupulous employers even bought up depreciated notes and palmed them off on their workingmen at face value. And, in the larger economic picture, all the stable-income classes had to stand by helpless and impotent during the unpredictable rise and fall of prices or ebb and flow of credit. Their reaction to a gambling economy was not delight at the opening up of chances for gain, but an intense feeling of insecurity. Jackson expressed their pent-up exasperation in his exclamation to the Baltimore committee on stockjobbers, brokers and gamblers — "would to God, they were all swept from the land!"[12]

The administration proposed to rescue the working classes from this treacherous economic order. "It is time," declared Taney, "that the just claims of this portion of society should be regarded in our legislation in relation to the currency. So far we have been providing facilities for those employed in extensive commerce, and have left the mechanic and the laborer to all the hazards of an insecure and unstable circulating medium." Jackson pronounced it "the duty of every government, so to regulate its currency as to protect this numerous class, as far as practicable, from the impositions of avarice and fraud."[13]

Prompted by these aims, the Jacksonians began to sketch out fairly coherent theories of self-generating business cycles. Condy Raguet was perhaps the first to adumbrate the general theory, and Gouge set forth the classic description in his *Paper Money*.

In its simplest outline the theory was this: Banks incline to over-issue their notes. Prices then rise, and a speculative fever begins to spread. Excited by the appearance of prosperity that accompanies boom, people spend freely. The general expansion of credit leads to overtrading and inflation. Every new business operation on credit creates more promissory notes, and these increase the demand for discounts, till finally the currency depreciates so greatly that specie is required for export in order to pay foreign debts. With specie at a premium, contraction sets in. Banks call in their loans, timid people start runs on banks, contraction turns to panic, and panic to collapse. "One man is unable to pay his debts," wrote Gouge. "His creditor de-

---

[11] *House Report*, 22 Congress 1 Session, no. 460, "Bank of the United States," 362, 364, 365, 367.

[12] See also his remark to the Philadelphia delegation that *"brokers and stock speculators, and all who were doing business upon borrowed capital . . . all such people ought to break." Niles' Register*, March 1, 8, 1834.

[13] Taney, "Letter to the Ways and Means Committee," April 15, 1834, *Register of Debates*, 23 Congress 1 Session, Appendix, 161; Richardson, comp., *Messages and Papers*, III, 302.

pended on him for the means of paying a third person to whom he is himself indebted. The circle extends through society. Multitudes become bankrupt, and a few successful speculators get possession of the earnings and savings of many of their frugal and industrious neighbors."[14]

The more careful analysts pointed out the complex interdependence of bank credit and general business activity, but political pamphleteers skipped the subtleties and blamed depressions on the paper-money system alone. Bank paper, they argued, stimulated the original boom psychology by beguiling businessmen into overtrading at times of rising prices. It linked the whole system so intimately that the failure of one merchant might prevent a dozen others from meeting their obligations. And most particularly, the expansion or contraction of paper in circulation bore only a perverse and futile relation to actual business needs. In the words of George Bancroft, it "expands when rising prices require a check to enterprise, and contracts when falling prices make credit most desirable." Or, as Theophilus Fisk put it with more venom, "The moment a spirit of speculation can be excited, the banks increase the flame by pouring oil upon it; the instant a reaction takes place, they add to the distress a thousand fold."[15]

If by modern standards highly inadequate, this currency theory of depression yet represented a considerable advance over no theory at all. Very little was then

said of general overproduction as a cause of depression. Some men, like Robert Rantoul, Jr., laid special stress on the glutting of markets as a factor in crisis; but many would agree with Gouge's note on such arguments, that "if the real wants of the community, and not their ability to pay, be considered, it will not, perhaps, be found that any one useful trade or profession has too many members," and accept his emphasis on the problem of "ability to pay." In 1843 Orestes A. Brownson in a brilliant passage placed the blame squarely on "our vicious method of distributing the products of labor." "More can be produced, in any given year," he wrote, "with the present productive power, than can be sold in any given five years." The fault lies in distribution.

We create a surplus — that is a surplus, not when we consider the wants of the people, but when we consider the state of the markets — and then must slacken our hand till the surplus is worked off. During this time, while we are working off the surplus, while the mills run short time, or stop altogether, the workmen must want employment. The evil is inherent in the system.

But this line of thought evidently failed to strike much response and was carried no farther.[16]

4

The political argument — opposition to the rise of independent powers within the state — had general premises deeply entrenched in the national consciousness. Everyone, from right to left, believed, with more or fewer qualifications, that

[14] Gouge, *Paper Money*, Part I, 24–25. See also Condy Raguet in the *Free Trade Advocate*, July 4, 1829, and the admirable discussion in Miller, *Banking Theories*, 192–203.

[15] George Bancroft, *Address at Hartford*, . . . *Feb. 18, 1840*, 14; Theophilus Fisk, *The Banking Bubble Burst; or the Mammoth Corruptions of the Paper Money System Relieved by Bleeding*, 25.

[16] Robert Rantoul, Jr., speech at Salem, March 31, 1834, Luther Hamilton, *Memoirs, Speeches and Writings of Robert Rantoul, Jr.*, 537; Gouge, *Paper Money*, Part I, 27–28; O. A. Brownson, "The Present State of Society," *Democratic Review*, XIII, 34 (July, 1843); see also O. A. Brownson, *Address on Social Reform*, 5–6.

sovereignty belonged to the people. It was but one step from this to declare that the people's government, therefore, should not be defied by private institutions; and it was easy to extend this proposition to economic institutions, as well as political.

In their nature as corporations, banks gave rise to one set of objections, springing from their monopoly of financial prerogative through special charter. Indeed, they provided so much the most flagrant instances of abuse of corporate privilege that they were mainly responsible for fixing national attention on the problem.

Their power over the currency was viewed as an especially grave encroachment on the domain of government. The regulation of the currency, in the words of Benton, was "one of the highest and most delicate acts of sovereign power . . . precisely equivalent to the power to create currency"; and he considered it "too great a power to be trusted to any banking company whatever, or to any authority but the highest and most responsible which was known to our form of Government." Commercial credit was another matter, "an affair of trade," as Cambreleng put it, "and not of government"; and the logic of this position pointed to the abolition of banks of note issue, on the one hand, and the establishment of free competition among banks of discount and deposit, on the other. The crucial error of the federal government, according to the hard-money advocates, lay in accepting bank notes in the payment of federal dues, by which it thus extended and virtually underwrote the credit of the banks. The remedy was to exclude bank notes from government payments.[17]

17 Benton in the Senate, March 22, 1834, *Register of Debates*, 23 Congress 1 Session, 1092–1093; Cambreleng to Van Buren, November 2,

The behavior of banks in practice, moreover, violated the national faith in popular rule. The most powerful argument against Biddle's Bank was always its calm assumption of independence. "The Bank of the United States," Jackson charged, "is in itself a Government which has gradually increased in strength from the day of its establishment. The question between it and the people has become one of power." Biddle's conduct, in 1834, in refusing to allow a House committee to investigate the Bank records or examine the Bank officers, was simply the climax of his oft-expressed theory of the Bank's independence. "This powerful corporation, and those who defend it," as Taney said, without much exaggeration, "seem to regard it as an independent sovereignty, and to have forgotten that it owes any duties to the People, or is bound by any laws but its own will."[18]

But Biddle was simply exhibiting on a larger scale habits long established in banking experience. William Graham Sumner concisely summed up the pretensions of the banks: —

The bankers had methods of doing things which were customary and conventional, but . . . contrary both to ordinary morality and to law as applied to similar matters outside of banks. . . . The banks also disregarded law so habitually that it became a commonplace that law could not bind them. . . . We search almost in vain through the law reports for any decisions on the rights or authority of the State over banks or the duties of banks to the State. It may be said

1835, Van Buren Papers. Cf. Gouge, *Paper Money*, Part I, 53: "The regulation of the currency is one of the most important prerogatives of sovereignty. This prerogative is now, in point of fact, surrendered to the Banks."

18 Jackson's first draft of the "Paper Read to the Cabinet," Jackson, *Correspondence*, V, 194; *Washington Globe*, October 1, 1834.

that no attempts were made to test or enforce the right of the State against banks,
and that, as a matter of practice, it had none.
The banks were almost irresponsible. Such
decisions as bear at all on the authority of
the State over banks proceed from the attempts of the banks to resist the exercise of
any authority whatever.

Such a situation obviously could not be
long borne. As Theophilus Fisk put it,
"Either the State is sovereign, or the
Banks are."[19]

5

The social argument — the battle
against domination by "the rich and
powerful" — represented the culmination
of the hard-money doctrine. The economic and political arguments, though
capable of standing by themselves, were
ultimately directed at conditions prelim-
inary to the question: who shall rule in
the state? The recurrent economic crises
were evil, not only in themselves, but
because they facilitated a redistribution
of wealth that built up the moneyed aristocracy. The irresponsible political sov-
ereignties were evil, not only in themselves, but because they provided the
aristocracy with instruments of power
and places of refuge.

The Bank War compelled people to
speculate once again about the conflict
of class. "There are but two parties," exclaimed Thomas Hart Benton, giving the
period its keynote; "there never has been
but two parties . . . founded in the radical question, whether PEOPLE, or PROP-
ERTY, shall govern? Democracy implies
a government by the people. . . . Aristocracy implies a government of the rich . . .
and in these words are contained the sum
of party distinction."[20]

The paper banking system was considered to play a leading role in this ever-
lasting struggle. Men living by the issue
and circulation of paper money produced
nothing; they added nothing to the national income; yet, they flourished and
grew wealthy. Their prosperity, it was
argued, must be stolen from the proceeds
of productive labor — in other words,
from the honest but defenseless "humble
members of society"; and Gouge exten-
sively annotated the modes of plunder.

The system was further important in
the strategy of the warfare. Taney described the big Bank as "the centre, and
the citadel of the moneyed power." "A
national bank," declared the Massachusetts Democratic convention of 1837, "is
the bulwark of the aristocracy; its out-
post, and its rallying point. It is the bond
of union for those who hold that Government should rest on property."[21] To a
lesser degree all banks acted as strong-
holds of conservatism. They provided the
funds and often the initiative for combat.
Their lawyers, lobbyists and newspapers
were eternally active. Politicians would
gather in their board rooms and consult
their presidents and accept gifts of stock.
More than any other kind of corporate
enterprise, banks boldly intervened in
politics when they felt their interests
menaced.

The hard-money policy attacked both
the techniques of plunder and the general strategy of warfare. By doing away
with paper money, it proposed to restrict
the steady transfer of wealth from the
farmer and laborer to the business community. By limiting banks to commercial
credit and denying them control over the
currency, it proposed to lessen their influence and power. By reducing the proportion of paper money, it proposed to

[19] Sumner, *History of Banking in the United
States*, 351–352; Fisk, *Banking Bubble Burst*, 72.

[20] *Niles' Register*, August 29, 1835.

[21] *Washington Globe*, August 25, 1834, October
27, 1837.

moderate the business cycle, and order the economy to the advantage of the worker rather than the speculator. It was a coherent policy, based on the best economic thought of the day, and formulated on a higher intellectual level than the alternatives of the opposition.

By origin and interest, it was a policy which appealed mainly to the submerged classes of the East and to the farmers of the South rather than to the frontier. Historians have too long been misled by the tableau of Jackson, the wild backwoodsman, erupting into the White House. In fact, the hard-money doctrine, which was not at all a frontier doctrine, was the controlling policy of the administration from the winter of 1833 on; and for some time it had been the secret goal of a small group, led by Jackson, Taney, Benton and Kendall, and passively encouraged by Van Buren. From the removal of the deposits to the end of Van Buren's presidency in 1840 this clique of radical Democrats sought to carry out the policy in its full implications. As soon as the hard-money program was divorced from the glamour of the Hero of New Orleans and had to rest on its inherent appeal, it did very badly in the West.

Andrew Jackson ably summed up its broad aims. "The planter, the farmer, the mechanic, and the laborer," he wrote, "all know that their success depends upon their own industry and economy, and that they must not expect to become suddenly rich by the fruits of their toil." These classes "form the great body of the people of the United States; they are the bone and sinew of the country." Yet "they are in constant danger of losing their fair influence in the Government." Why? "The mischief springs from the power which the money interest derives from a paper currency, which they are able to control, from the multitude of corporations with exclusive privileges which they have succeeded in obtaining in the different States." His warning to his people was solemn. "Unless you become more watchful . . . you will in the end find that the most important powers of Government have been given or bartered away, and the control over your dearest interests has passed into the hands of these corporations."[22]

6

Taney and Benton worked out the details of the immediate hard-money measures. They proposed to increase the metallic basis of the currency in two directions: by the restoration of gold to circulation, and by the suppression of small notes. The first measure had been for many years close to Benton's heart. Gold had long been undervalued, at the ratio of 15 to 1, with the result that no gold eagles and only a scattering of other gold coins had been minted since 1805, and most of these rapidly left the country. Benton argued that, if the gold were not thus expelled, the amount of specie derivable from foreign commerce, added to the amount obtained from American mines, could supply all financial needs without recourse to small notes or "shinplasters."[23] In June, 1834, his bill to revise the valuation to 16 to 1 passed Congress. As an expression of the strictly economic intentions of the hard-money policy, it made a broad appeal to all men of good will, winning the support of John Quincy Adams, Webster and Calhoun. Only diehards like Clay and Horace Binney opposed it.

22 Richardson, comp., *Messages and Papers*, III, 305–306.

23 See Benton's great speech on the gold currency, in the Senate, March 21–22, 1834, *Register of Debates*, 23 Congress 1 Session, especially 1073–1084; Benton, *Thirty Years' View*, I, 436–457.

The change in the coinage ratio was one of Benton's greatest triumphs. He exulted in the new flow of gold to the government mints. "This is the money the Constitution provides," he would say, "and I will not have anything to do with any other kind." Or, in another mood, "What! Do you want a coroner's jury to sit and say, 'Old Bullion died of shinplasters?'"[24] Old Bullion was the name his hard-money fixation had won him, among his friends, at least; his enemies called him sarcastically the Gold Humbug. For a time, foes of the hard-money policy sought to ridicule Benton's reform out of existence. Gilt counters were circulated, with grotesque figures and caustic inscriptions — the "whole hog" and the "better currency." But no one dared argue directly that this infusion of specie would not improve the health of the economy.

The effects of revaluation were immediate. Levi Woodbury reported in December, 1836, that more gold had been coined in the twelve months preceding than in the first sixteen years of the mint's existence, and more in the two and a half years since revaluation than in the thirty-one before. In October, 1833, there had been only thirty million dollars of specie in the country, of which twenty-six million was in banks. In December, 1836, there was seventy-three million dollars, of which only forty-five million was in banks.[25]

Yet the revival of gold would hardly be enough without measures to suppress small notes. This proposal had the sanction, not only of the theory of Adam Smith (and of Nicholas Biddle), but of the example of Great Britain, which had established a £5 minimum in 1829. Most economically literate conservatives acknowledged the theoretical advantages of suppression;[26] and Congress and the Treasury, drawing on their authority to define the kind of money receivable in federal payments, could exert real, if limited, influence on the issues of state banks. A joint resolution of 1816 had made all notes from specie-paying banks acceptable in tax payments. In a Treasury circular of April, 1835, all notes under $5 were banned, and banks holding government deposits were forbidden to issue such notes. In February, 1836, a similar circular banned notes under $10, and a congressional act of April, 1836, prohibited notes under $20 after March 3, 1837, and required immediate convertibility for all notes. The conditions imposed on the deposit banks controlled their stock transactions, as well as their note issue, calling for weekly statements and ordering that they should always be open for examination. Declared Secretary Woodbury, "All mystery on the subject of banking should cease."[27]

---

24 Meigs, *Benton*, 263.

25 Levi Woodbury, "Report from the Secretary of the Treasury," December 6, 1836, *Register of Debates*, 24 Congress 2 Session, Appendix, 79. It is hard to assess the hard-money claim that specie could have altogether displaced small notes. Gouge calculated in 1841 that "barely by detaining in the country such amounts of gold and silver as come to us in the present course of trade, we should, in ten or twelve years, have a perfectly sound circulating medium." *Journal of Banking*, December 22, 1841. Whether or not

one-hundred-per-cent displacement was possible, or desirable, an increase in the proportion of specie was badly needed.

26 Some conservatives would argue of shinplasters, however, like a Massachusetts committee in 1840, "They float as free as the snow flakes, and every hand is held out to catch as much as it can of the beneficial shower. If they were found to be unsafe or inconvenient, they would instantly be rejected." Massachusetts *House Document*, no. 66 (1840), 5.

27 Levi Woodbury, "Report on the Present System of Keeping and Disbursing the Public Money," December 12, 1834, *Register of Debates*, 23 Congress 2 Session, Appendix, 105.

But these regulations had little effect on the general banking situation. Only by deliberately rousing public opinion within the states could the administration hope to abolish small notes. In some states tattered shinplasters circulated with face values of 12½ or even 6¼ cents. In December, 1834, Jackson appealed to the states to follow the national example. Pennsylvania, Maryland and Virginia already had legislation against small bills. In 1835 Maine, Connecticut and New York outlawed notes below $5, while North Carolina, Georgia, Alabama, Ohio, Indiana and Missouri also passed restrictive measures.[28]

7

But the administration's campaign came too late. The wise counsels of the hard-money advocates were drowned out by the roar of the nation's greatest boom in years. The Bank of the United States alone enlarged its loans an average of two and a half million dollars a month and its paper circulation by a total of ten million dollars between December, 1834, and July, 1835.[29] Smaller banks rushed to follow, increasing the amount of paper money from eighty-two million dollars on January 1, 1835, to one hundred and eight million, a year later, and one hundred and twenty million by December 1, 1836.[30]

Wages climbed, opportunity seemed limitless and riches appeared to lie everywhere. A popular tract of 1836 — *The Book of Wealth; in Which It Is Proved*

from the Bible, that It Is the Duty of Every Man to Become Rich — suggests the temper of the day. Designed to allay any religious misgivings about joining at the trough, the book earnestly declared one thing to be certain: "no man can be obedient to God's will as revealed in the Bible, without, as the general result, becoming wealthy."[31]

The administration watched the speculative mania with profound alarm. In the *Globe* Frank Blair repeatedly voiced the deep anxieties of the hard-money circle. "We have again and again warned the community," he wrote in the spring of 1835, "of the infatuation which had seized them since the panic, to embark in every species of extravagant speculation." A month later: "this state of things cannot last. . . . A reaction is as certain to take place as the sun is to continue its diurnal course." After a year of similar remarks: "The only remedy is to be found in banking less and trading less."[32]

Jackson, in the early months of 1836, lifted his voice in conversation against "the mad career" in which the nation was rushing to ruin. Benton declared angrily in the Senate: "I did not join in putting down the Bank of the United States, to put up a wilderness of local banks. I did not join in putting down the paper currency of a national bank, to put up a national paper currency of a thousand local banks. I did not strike Caesar," he concluded in magnificent wrath, "to make Anthony master of Rome. . . . The present bloat in the paper system cannot continue. . . . The revulsion will come, as surely as it did in 1819–'20." When

---

[28] D. R. Dewey, *State Banking before the Civil War*, 68–71.

[29] *Washington Globe,* June 10, 1835, May 12, 1836.

[30] Levi Woodbury, "Report from the Secretary of the Treasury," December 6, 1836, *Register of Debates,* 24 Congress 2 Session, Appendix, 80.

[31] Thomas P. Hunt, *The Book of Wealth,* 5, 22, 24.

[32] *Washington Globe,* May 23, June 10, 1835, May 31, 1836.

Secretary Woodbury made his report in December, 1836, he had to predict that the inflation would "produce much distress, embarrassment, and ruin, before this specie can be duly equalized, the excesses of paper sufficiently curtailed, and the exorbitant discounts gradually lessened."[33]

A basic cause of the inflation was land speculation, and the administration had already moved to plug up this great hole in the national economy. The receivability of bank notes in payment for the public lands had practically converted the national domain into a fund for the redemption of the notes, providing in effect a capital for seven or eight hundred institutions to bank on, and filling the Treasury with more or less worthless paper. Benton had pointed out in detail how land sales passed on to the government the job of underwriting the whole banking system. Speculators would borrow five, ten, twenty, fifty thousand dollars in paper from banks on the condition of using it on the frontier. They would then pay the notes to government land offices in exchange for land, which served as security for additional loans; meanwhile, the notes circulated freely as land-office money, some never returning to the original bank for redemption, the rest only after a long interval. This racket not only subsidized the banking interest — land sales had risen from four million dollars a year to five million a quarter — but it also, in Benton's words, irretrievably entangled "the federal Government with the ups and downs of the whole

paper system, and all the fluctuations, convulsions, and disasters, to which it was subject."[34]

Benton introduced a resolution requiring that the public lands be paid for in specie. Webster, with his usual policy of supporting sound money except when concrete measures were proposed which might secure it, led the attack on this measure, and a combination of Whigs and conservative Democrats killed it in the Senate. But after adjournment Jackson had Benton draw up an executive order embodying his idea, and the famous "Specie Circular" was issued.

The business community grew furious over this latest evidence of executive despotism. When Congress reassembled in December, the Whigs demanded the repeal of the Circular and the reopening of the land offices to wildcat money, and the Democrats split wide under the pressure. One wing, led by William Cabell Rives of Virginia and N. P. Tallmadge of New York, emerged as defenders of the state banks. Benton vainly urged the imminence of a financial explosion which would leave the Treasury holding the bag; but his efforts won him little more than denunciation as "that most miserable Jacobin of the woods of Missouri, who, with an impudence and insolence unparalleled, has attempted to overthrow the commercial and financial relations and institutions of this country."[35] The final vote disclosed a tiny group of five men, led by Benton and Silas Wright, upholding the hard-money position. The bill passed the House and went to the President on the day before adjournment.

---

[33] Jackson's conversation reported by "A Yeoman," *Washington Globe*, August 11, 1837; Benton in the Senate, January 27, 1837, *Register of Debates*, 24 Congress 2 Session, 610; Levi Woodbury, "Report from the Secretary of the Treasury," December 6, 1836, *Register of Debates*, 24 Congress 2 Session, Appendix, 80.

[34] Benton in the Senate, April 23, 1836, *Register of Debates*, 24 Congress 1 Session, 1255–1257. See also *Washington Globe*, July 12, 1836.

[35] *Boston Commercial Gazette*, February 27, 1837.

Firm to the end, the old General returned it with his veto.

Jackson thus had to overrule Congress to sustain the hard-money policy. But the Specie Circular furnished the only tense financial issue in the last years of his administration. After the panic session the great scenes of battle began to shift to the states. Here, in places inaccessible to the long arm and grim energy of General Jackson, little bands of devoted Jacksonians fought to stem the rush for bank and corporate charters, unfolding the potentialities of the Jacksonian program, enriching the techniques and amplifying the intellectual resources.

Above all, these local battles called forth the common people in cities, towns and country — the poor day laborer, the industrious mechanic, the hard-handed farmer — the "humble members of society" everywhere. They listened for hours on hot summer days to dry expositions of financial policy. They crowded in bare and unheated halls on cold winter nights to hear about the evils of banking. They read, and thumbed, and passed along tracts and speeches attacking the paper system. They saw the dizzy climb of prices, wages lagging behind, raged silently at discounted bank notes, and wondered at the behavior of Democratic politicians pledged against voting for incorporations. They talked among themselves, with shrewdness and good sense and alarm. . . . Their discontent was real and widespread. It found its leaders, and the experience of these years prepared them for one great final drive on the national scene.

Bray Hammond: PUBLIC POLICY AND NATIONAL BANKS

MR. Schlesinger's book is important and abounds in excellences: it deals with a significant period, it is comprehensive in its interest, and it is entertainingly written. Mr. Schlesinger has a fine talent for peopling an epoch vividly. But his book is marred by two faults. One is a Manichaean naïveté with respect to the nobility of all things Jacksonian and the sordidness of all things opposed. The other is a fumbling treatment of economic matters and particularly of the Bank of the United States.

Mr. Schlesinger's vocabulary purrs over his friends. The landscapes at the Hermitage and Kinderhook smile in a fashion not noticeable where Whigs and Federalists live. The Jacksonian leaders have a "pervading insight," their wrath is "magnificent," one or another of them is "handsome," "grave," "masterly," "erudite," "thoughtful," "quiet," "intelligent," "brilliant," etc., etc., and the old hero himself is touchingly fond of children. The opposition is a sorry outfit. They are Bank "lackeys," they "roar" and "snarl," they deal in "hullabaloo," they are "phony," they have "fantasies," they work "backstairs," their best minds are "opaque," and one gets the impression that Mr. Schlesinger never thinks of them as loving little children at all. Jackson's trick of evading awkward questions by simulating an apoplectic rage that filled his visitors with fear lest the aged president burst a blood vessel on their account is described with affectionate amusement and admiration. The immense services of Hamilton to his country are disregarded. The reader is allowed to look at Van Buren only through high-powered magnifying glasses. Marshall and Story are written down with casual finality, and Taney is promoted as if no dissent existed; Webster is about the only member of Mr. Schlesinger's flock of goats whose defense he bothers to notice.

The Bank war is properly very important in Mr. Schlesinger's account, and yet he does not make the Bank of the United States a clearly functioning financial institution nor Nicholas Biddle a central banker with specific monetary policies and programs that can be appraised. Instead he makes the Bank a dim sort of moneyed monstrosity and Biddle a vague, sinister figure, "drunk with power," whose career is a darkened background for Jackson's gleaming achievements. This makes poor history. The Bank of the United States was a central bank and should be discussed as such. But Mr. Schlesinger never uses the term, never mentions the purposes for which the Bank was set up, and never but casually speaks of its functions as public in their nature. He says it was "privately controlled"; but so was the Bank of England

This review of Schlesinger's *The Age of Jackson* is reprinted from *The Journal of Economic History*, 6 (May, 1946), 79–84, by permission of the New York University Press.

and so was practically every other similar institution till recent times. He speaks of the Bank's "profitable relations with the government" as if they were one-sided. He even says the Bank "allowed the government to appoint" five directors — a preposterous statement that may be intended for sarcasm but will be taken by most readers at face value. One might as well assert that the Treasury, for example, or any other government department "allows" the President and Congress to say who shall be at its head; for it was by authority of an act of Congress creating the Bank that the government directors were appointed by the President, with confirmation by the Senate.

That the Bank was a public institution formed at the instance of the government and for its convenience, that under Biddle's management it performed its depository services efficiently, furnished a sound and uniform currency, and regulated the state banks, and that the state banks and their borrowers resented its restraint upon credit — these are facts that the Jacksonians liked to ignore. It is less excusable to ignore them now, for they are facts that Gallatin, Dunbar, Catterall, Dewey, and other scholars, on the basis of known information, long ago put outside the field of intelligent controversy. Mr. Schlesinger does not wholly ignore them, but he mentions them in an offhand way as if they had no special significance. "In destroying the Bank," he says, "Jackson had removed a valuable brake on credit expansion; and in sponsoring the system of deposit in state banks he had accelerated the tendencies toward inflation." Mr. Schlesinger glides over startling facts like these, unstartled; and recognizes no need to reconcile them with his general picture of the Bank as an outlaw institution, obscurely dangerous because it "had too much power."

As to the reality of this power, "there could be no question," he says; and he goes clear out on the limb to say that the Bank "enjoyed a virtual monopoly of the currency and practically complete control over credit and the price level." This is sheer romance. Mr. Schlesinger contradicts himself to indulge in it, for he often speaks elsewhere of the currency issues of the local banks, clearly implying thereby that no "monopoly" existed. In reality, of course, the Bank furnished about a quarter of the total paper circulation. As for "practically complete control over credit," the Bank had nothing of the sort, nor has any central bank ever achieved it, even though it should. As for "practically complete" control of the price level, the idea is ridiculous; it would be hard to surpass its utter detachment from the findings of price analysts and historians, to say nothing of common sense. But Mr. Schlesinger leaves the solid earth frequently, in little things as well as big. For example, he speaks of the Bank's "alacrity in opening new offices" in 1831 and 1832 while renewal of the charter was pending, as conclusive evidence, in Taney's words, of its determination to fasten itself on the country. R. C. H. Catterall found "not a grain of evidence" to support such charges, and no one has produced any since. Far from showing "alacrity" in opening new offices, the Bank established none after 1830, in which year it established the last four of the twenty-nine it had in all; of these, all but ten had been set up during the Bank's initial organization in 1817.

Mr. Schlesinger's failure to make proper use of the work of scholars who have written authoritatively on the Bank seems to me inexplicable. I found reference to Mr. Catterall on only one point of fact, and the whole body of Catterall's judicious and thorough work is neglected for a superficial presentation scarcely above the level of Mr. Marquis James's unpenetrating account in his *Life of Jackson*. I had rather Mr. Schlesinger had shown no knowledge of Catterall whatever; for then he would have spared a reviewer the painful effort to understand how he could revive Benton's pomposities about the branch drafts without remarking Catterall's disposal of the question fifty years ago. The same is true of Dewey, who confirmed Catterall, and of Gallatin, whose unimpeachable contemporary testimony clearly indicates the public nature of the Bank, Biddle's good performance before Jackson's attack, the want of justification for that attack, and the degeneration of Biddle after his failure to withstand the attack.

Mr. Schlesinger makes much of the distinction that although the Jacksonians were understood to be opposed to all banks, they really opposed only the note-issue function and not the deposit function. He devotes an appendix to this point and seems to consider it creditable to the Jacksonians, as if it showed how well they understood banking. The opposite is what it shows. For the differences between note and deposit liabilities are only those of form, and one is as capable of mischief as the other. When Mr. Schlesinger quotes Gallatin to show that banking in the United States was universally understood to mean note issue, he should quote the same authority to the effect that there was not "the slightest difference" between note and deposit liabilities — and incidentally he should enjoy making Webster contradict himself by saying not only that note issue was the essential function of banking but also that it was "not an indispensable ingredient" of banking. Mr. Schlesinger has loyally picked up the Jacksonian confusion on this matter. The actual result

of the program he praises was to free both the note and deposit functions from regulation — a blunder that the National Bank Act in 1863 and the Federal Reserve Act fifty years later both purposed to undo.

Mr. Schlesinger properly emphasizes the fact that Jacksonian democracy reflected eastern as well as frontier influences, but it seems to me that he errs in associating the eastern influence with labor alone and not with business enterprise. There was no more important factor in the Jacksonian movement than the democratization of business, which ceased thenceforth to be the *métier* of a predominantly mercantile, exclusive group, or commercial aristocracy, as it was in the days of Hamilton, and became an interest of the common man. This process of democratization went hand in hand with the rise of laissez faire. Mr. Schlesinger appears to see no break in the business tradition, and makes Hamilton represent it as much in 1840 as he did in 1790. But to identify business enterprise of 1840 with business enterprise of 1790, it is necessary to slur over too much — for example, the appeal of Jackson's politics to money-makers like Alexander Hamilton's own son, who was one of Jackson's supporters and advisers, and like Henshaw, who frankly wanted the United States Bank overthrown so that he and his friends might have room for a big bank of their own. It is also necessary to slur over the more general fact that the speculation which mounted to the panic of 1837 was a great popular phenomenon and reflected the current interests of Americans no less than did the labor and utopian movements of the time. Authentic and American as the latter were, they still were typical not of American behavior as a whole but rather of the idealistic rebellion of minorities against the rising spirit of free enterprise. For a brief period all the diverse dissatisfactions with the old order of things united behind the picturesque intransigence of Andrew Jackson, with this new, un-Hamiltonian spirit of free enterprise prominent and powerful among them. The honeymoon was brief, and in 1840 enterprise eloped with the Whigs. But while it was supporting Jackson, it had separated the corporate form of organization from monopoly and put forth the promise that anyone could be a capitalist, an investor, or a speculator; and it had made banking a form of business "free" and open to all. Business had become the citadel of rugged individualism, and American conservatism had become rooted not so much in Wall Street as in the breasts of rural capitalists and village entrepreneurs — to the recurring embarrassment of liberal and radical causes ever since.

In Hamilton's day business had been strongly federal, but it was now beginning to see advantages in states rights — a ground of opposition to the Bank that it seems to me Mr. Schlesinger neglects. The states'-rights argument had vigorously survived the Supreme Court's vindication of the Bank's constitutionality, thanks partly to strongly held principle, no doubt, but much more to selfish interest. Hence, in destroying the Bank, Mr. Schlesinger's hard-money horses played directly into the hands of the state banks and of the speculators they abominated. The local banks always called the regulatory measures of the Bank of the United States "coercion" and "oppression," and it was notorious that they wanted it out of the way. In state after state, as its end neared, the legislatures were jammed with charter applications. Benton's words, quoted by Mr. Schlesinger, sound pathetic: "I did not join in

putting down the Bank of the United States to put up a wilderness of local banks." He might disavow the purpose but not the deed.

The situation in the United States, with a rapidly growing and acquisitive population pressing to exploit immense resources, was one where the public interest required an extremely powerful restraint upon inflation. The Bank under the direction of Nicholas Biddle was applying that restraint. Jackson, since he abhorred speculation, should have corrected and fostered the Bank. Instead he identified it with the evil it was contending against, a bank being simply a bank to him, destroyed it, and delivered the country to the excesses of a disordered currency and unregulated credit expansion. I do not find fault with him for attacking economic privilege; I find fault with him for *thinking* he was attacking it when in fact he was attacking a semi-governmental institution that restrained speculation. His action was calamitous for a people who were entering a fierce and trampling struggle for conversion of the virgin earth into private property and erection of still more property upon it — a lasting struggle in which the objects of Jacksonian concern have had the most to suffer. Nor should I be fond enough to believe that a central bank or any other governmental instrumentality could have prevented that struggle; but it might have tempered it. And it is significant that today the party interests to which Mr. Schlesinger is allegiant turn to central banking as a first means of accomplishing their social aims. To suggest that the Jacksonians might have sought to nationalize the Bank of the United States as the Bank of England and the Bank of France have recently been would be historically fantastic, but one may question the sagacity of those who went so far in the opposite direction as to destroy the central bank just when it began to be needed most. That action may be excused but cannot properly be praised.

Mr. Schlesinger's book will be widely read; and because its documentation is profuse it will be considered authoritative by most of its readers. I do not think it should be so considered. It represents the age of Jackson as one of triumphant liberalism when it was as much or more an age of triumphant exploitation; it fosters a simplistic notion of continuing problems of human welfare; and it thickens the myths around a political leader who had more capacity for action than for accomplishment.

Suggestions for Additional Reading

Two good general financial histories of the United States are available to the reader desirous of reviewing the financial history of the young republic and attaining a better perspective from which to view the struggle over the rechartering of the second Bank of the United States. They are William J. Shultz and M. R. Caine, *Financial Development of the United States* (New York, 1937), and Davis R. Dewey, *Financial History of the United States* (New York, 1934). Both provide valuable bibliographical guides.

On the second Bank itself, the standard work is Ralph C. H. Catterall, *The Second Bank of the United States* (Chicago, 1903). Although further light has been shed on the Bank since this book was published nearly fifty years ago, and the reader may not agree with all of Catterall's evaluations, yet no serious student can afford to overlook this scholarly and exhaustive study. Much briefer, but a good summary based largely on Catterall's findings, is Davis R. Dewey, "The Second Bank of the United States," *The First and Second Banks of the United States, Senate Document*, 61 Congress, 2 Session, Vol. 26 (1909–1910), pp. 147–265.

A most valuable recent study of the Bank War is to be found in Fritz Redlich, *The Molding of American Banking Men and Ideas* (New York, 1947), pp. 96–186. Redlich analyzes with great care and considerable insight the roles played by Biddle and Jackson, giving unusual attention not only to the technical banking issues but to the larger economic and social problems.

Especially useful for the political and personal side of the controversy, though sometimes less so on the economic and financial issues involved, are biographies of the leading figures in the controversy. Among the best of these are Carl B. Swisher, *Roger B. Taney* (New York, 1935); Marquis James, *Andrew Jackson, Portrait of a President* (New York, 1937); and Claude M. Fuess, *Daniel Webster* (Boston, 1930). To these should be added the lively account in Claude G. Bowers, *The Party Battles of the Jackson Period* (Boston, 1922).

Of the abundant literature produced at the time of the Bank War much is easily available to the student but only a few of the more important items can be mentioned here. The letters of the two leading figures are available respectively in Reginald C. McGrane, *The Correspondence of Nicholas Biddle* (Boston, 1919), and John S. Bassett, *Correspondence of Andrew Jackson* (Washington, 1935). For the congressional phase of the struggle a good anti-Bank summary will be found in Thomas H. Benton, *Thirty Years' View* (New York, 1854), pp. 220–291. But the student will wish to go either to their collected works or to the *Register of Debates in Congress* to consult important speeches by such pro-Bank leaders as Webster, Clay, and McDuffie. A detailed examination of the whole financial situation and a defense of the Bank will be found in Henry

Adams, ed., *The Writings of Albert Gallatin* (Philadelphia, 1879), III, 235–364. George Tucker, *The Theory of Money and Banks Investigated* (Boston, 1839), provides an excellent summary of the chief arguments as viewed by a contemporary admirer of the Bank.

Finally, in order to get some feeling for the flavor and heat of the debate, the student may wish to do some browsing in old newspapers, especially for the year 1832, if they are available. Practically all contain editorials or communications on this issue, but especially useful are two Washington, D. C., newspapers, the *National Intelligencer* for the Bank and the *Washington Globe* against it.